Branch Lines of Devon

Plymouth, West and North Devon

Branch Lines of Devon

Plymouth, West and North Devon

COLIN G. MAGGS

ALAN SUTTON PUBLISHING LIMITED

First published in the United Kingdom in 1995
Alan Sutton Publishing Limited · Phoenix Mill · Stroud · Gloucestershire

British Library Cataloguing-in-Publication Data.

Maggs, Colin G.
Branch Lines of Devon. -Plymouth, West
and North Devon
I. Title
385.094235

ISBN 0-7509-0720-7

Endpapers. Front: 43XX class 2–6–0 No. 6398 at Venn Cross with a Down goods train. The station offices can be seen above the signal-box roof. On the far right is the end of the goods shed. Smoke and steam are coming from the 246 yd Venn Cross Tunnel. (21.6.58, R.J. Sellick)
Back: A 55XX class 2–6–2T carrying express headlights with a Down train at Acland Cross, Landkey, between Swimbridge and Barnstaple. *(c.* 1928, A. Halls)

Typeset in 10/12 Palatino.
Typesetting and origination by
Alan Sutton Publishing Limited.
Printed and bound in Great Britain by
Butler & Tanner Ltd, Frome, Somerset.

Contents

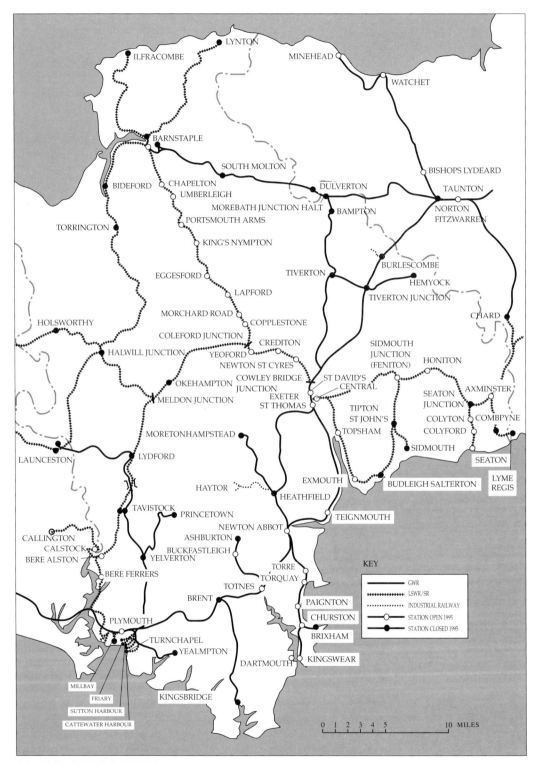

KEY

———————— GWR
+++++++++ LSWR/SR
·············· INDUSTRIAL RAILWAY
○ STATION OPEN 1995
● STATION CLOSED 1995

BRANCH LINES OF DEVON

vi

Introduction

The railway map of Devon has a simple basic pattern. In the 1840s the allies of the broad gauge Great Western Railway, the Bristol & Exeter Railway and the South Devon Railway, thrust the main line forward to Plymouth. The broad gauge faction did not hold its monopoly for long. In 1860 the London & South Western Railway opened to Exeter and pushed on to Barnstaple. East of this line the GWR held sway in the north of the county and the LSWR in the south, while to the west of the Exeter to Barnstaple line matters were reversed. Both companies had branches in the Plymouth area, some serving various docks both for freight and passengers and mail from liners.

A few branches in Devon were considered main lines. The Norton Fitzwarren to Barnstaple branch was marked as such by the GWR on its maps, doubtless with the intent to impress potential Ilfracombe traffic. The former LSWR line between Exeter and Barnstaple used to be a main line, but is now relegated to branch status. Only the ends of the former main line between Coleford Junction and Plymouth exist, as the Meldon Quarry branch and the southern end of the Callington and Gunnislake line.

After the conversion of the final broad gauge in May 1892, the LSWR and GWR could use several alternative routes between Plymouth, Exeter and London – a useful arrangement when one was blocked through accident, landslip, storm or flood.

The first railway in the area was the 4 ft 6 in gauge horse-worked Plymouth & Dartmoor Railway, opened in 1823. Principally it carried stone from Princetown to Plymouth and coal, lime and timber in the reverse direction.

Although the western half of Devon lost many of its branches in the closures of the 1950s and '60s, two remain open for passengers, to Barnstaple and Gunnislake. The Plym Valley Railway is a preserved line. Meldon Quarry–Coleford Junction is still important as it carries a heavy tonnage of railway ballast.

Generally the ex-LSWR branches are described first and then those of the GWR. In both cases the order is anti-clockwise.

Grateful thanks are due to P. Burkhalter for checking the section on the Devonport Dockyard Railway (he is the author of a book on the subject, to be published by Twelveheads Press) and to E.J.M. Hayward for checking and improving the whole text and captions.

Key to all maps

————	Great Western Railway
++++++++++	London & South Western/Southern Railway
············	Industrial railway

Brent to Kingsbridge

As there was easy access to Kingsbridge by sea, the town did not feature in early railway schemes. A local company obtained an Act of Parliament on 29 July 1864 and four miles of track were laid, but works were abandoned through shortage of capital, and the company's powers expired in due course.

The Kingsbridge & Salcombe Railway Act was granted on 24 July 1882. Its powers passed to the GWR by an Act of 13 August 1888, the latter company having raised the capital. The contractor for building the line was Charles Chambers. Salcombe was never reached but the single standard gauge line opened to Kingsbridge on 19 December 1893.

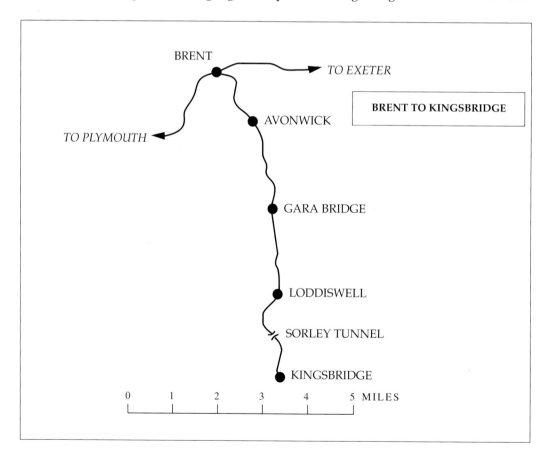

A 3101 class (later 44XX) 2–6–2T, heading the early morning mixed train to Kingsbridge, stands at the loop platform, Brent. The 4-wheel coaches are flat roofed. Notice the peeling paint on the smokebox door and the bridge rail in the sidings.

c. 1908 Lens of Sutton

Like many railways the branch suffered from road competition and it closed to passengers and goods on 16 September 1963.

The junction with the GWR's main line was at Brent, where branch trains used the outer face of the Down island platform, a run-round loop being situated between this and the goods shed.

On leaving the station the branch curved south-east down a gradient of 1 in 50, reaching the Avon and following it. Avonwick had a single platform with two stone buildings, the smaller being used as a goods shed. William Clarke was the engineer responsible for designing the attractive stations along the branch. The three ornate chimney stacks had either a pair or a trio of vertical stone deflectors. In 1866 Clarke had been appointed assistant chief engineer of the London & North Western Railway and the first line on which Clarke's standard station design appeared was the Bristol & North Somerset Railway between Bristol and Radstock in 1873. The Kingsbridge & Salcombe Railway was the last new line with which he was involved. The siding at Avonwick, used in recent years for a camping coach, closed on 11 June 1956, from which date the station was unstaffed.

Beyond Avonwick reverse curves carried the line through a densely wooded valley, crossing the Avon ten times. One salmon poacher arranged for the footplate crew to inform him by whistle code of the whereabouts of the water bailiff and suitably rewarded them. The buildings at Gara Bridge were identical with those at Avonwick but the track layout was different, as Gara Bridge had a passing loop and two platforms. The siding stabled a camping coach in summer. The building on the single platform at Loddiswell, about 200 ft below the village, was almost identical to that at Avonwick, and its siding, too, stabled camping coaches. The station closed to goods on 4 September 1961, from which date it was unstaffed.

Just beyond the station the branch left the Avon, rose at 1 in 50 through the 638 yd Sorley

Tunnel and, emerging from its southern portal, goods trains had to observe a stop board before the gradient changed to 1 in 50 down to Kingsbridge station, situated above, but close to, the town centre and quay. The station had a long, curving platform, a bay having been added on 15 August 1915. When the station building was enlarged around 1926, Clarke's style was retained. The carriage siding had a corrugated iron shed, which held two coaches. The goods yard included four roads, a large goods shed and cattle pens. Outward freight traffic comprised products from local mills, scrap iron, agricultural machinery and farm produce, and was substantial right up until the closure of the branch. The line was particularly busy in the weeks leading up to D-Day, as the coast at Slapton was used for training before the Normandy landings, and several special trains were run daily.

In the early days passenger traffic on the branch was worked by 517 class 0–4–2Ts and 'Metro' class 2–4–0Ts, with 1901 class 0–6–0STs handling goods traffic. After the First World War a 45XX class 2–6–2T appeared. Unlike on many GWR branches, autotrains were never run, though in 1910 a Plymouth steam railmotor made a through trip on Sundays. The stone-built shed, designed by Clarke, adjoined the bay platform at Kingsbridge. The station closed in September 1961.

In 1911 the branch passenger train consisted of the following coaches, all four-wheeled: brake third, third, composite brake third. Latterly trains consisted of two B-sets, a third class coach being added when strengthening was required. Some trains were 'mixed'. On summer Saturdays through coaches ran to and from Paddington and up to a thousand passengers arrived from various destinations.

The initial rail service in 1893 consisted of five trains each way and by 1910 this had increased to six trains and one on Sundays. The journey took 36 minutes for the 12½ miles. By 1938 the service had improved to eight Down and seven Up trains, with an additional two and one respectively on Saturdays. The timetable for the summer of 1961 showed six trains each way Mondays to Fridays, with an additional five Down and three Up on Saturdays. Speed was restricted to 35 mph.

The GWR inaugurated a bus service between Kingsbridge and Salcombe on 21 July 1909 and this ran until 31 December 1928, when the route was taken over by Western National Omnibus Company. The bus service connected with the trains.

Table 93	BRENT and KINGSBRIDGE (for Salcombe)																				
					WEEK DAYS ONLY																
Miles		am	am	am		pm	pm	pm		pm	pm		pm	pm		pm	pm		pm	pm	pm	pm
			S	E		E	S	S		S	B		E	S		S	E		S	E	S	
	Brent .. _ _ _ dep	8 20	9 48	10 10	..	12 24	12 34	1 20	..	2 10	3 40	..	4 15	4 38	..	5 20	5 35	..	6 10	6 50	7 10	9 20	..
2½	Avonwick _ _ _ _	8 27	9 54	10 16	..	12 30	12 40	1 27	..	2 17	3 47	..	4 22	4 46	..	5 27	5 42	..	6 17	6 57	7 17	9 27	..
5½	Gara Bridge. _ _	8 35	10 2	10 23	..	12 38	12 48	1 35	..	2 27	3 55	..	4 32	4 54	..	5 35	5 50	..	6 27	7 5	7 25	9 35	..
9	Loddiswell .. _ _ _	8 43	10 10	10 31	..	12 46	12 56	1 43	..	2 35	4 3	..	4 40	5 2	..	5 43	5 58	..	6 36	7 13	7 33	9 43	..
12½	Kingsbridge .. .. arr	8 55	10 25	10 46	..	12 58	1 8	1 55	..	2 50	4 15	..	4 52	5 15	..	5 55	6 10	..	6 50	7 30	7 45	9 54	..
—	Salcombe ¶ ...... arr	9 29	11 26	11 26	..	1 26	1 56	2 28	..	3 28	4 58	..	5 28	5 56	..	6 28	6 58	..	7 56	7 58	8 58	11 3	..

Miles		am		am	am	am	am	am		am		pm		pm		pm	pm		pm	pm	pm
				S	E	D	E	S		S				E		S	E		S	F	
—	Salcombe ¶ .. .. dep	6 55	..	8 27	..	10 0	..	10 30	10 30	..	11 30	..	1 30	..	3 30	..	4 0	4 30	..	5 0	5 30	7 0
—	Kingsbridge .. _ _ dep	7 26	..	9 5	9 25	10 55	..	11 0	11 15	..	12 50	..	2 10	..	4 15	..	4 35	5 15	..	5 30	5 50	7 50
3½	Loddiswell .. _ _ ..	7 36	..	9 15	9 35	..	..	11 8	11 25	..	12 40	..	2 20	..	4 25	..	4 45	5 25	..	5 40	..	8 0
7	Gara Bridge. _ _ _ _	7 43	..	9 22	9 42	..	..	11 16	11 32	..	12 50	..	2 27	..	4 33	..	4 53	5 35	..	5 50	..	8 8
10	Avonwick _ _ _ _ ..	7 52	..	9 30	9 50	..	..	11 24	11 40	..	12 58	..	2 35	..	4 42	..	5 0	5 43	..	5 58	..	8 15
12½	Brent .... arr	8 0	..	9 40	10 0	11 30	..	11 35	11 50	..	1 5	..	2 45	..	4 50	..	5 10	5 51	..	6 6	6 35	8 24

B Saturdays only. Through Carriages from London (Pad.) dep 11 0 am (Table 81)	D Saturdays only. Through Carriages to London (Pad.) arr 4 18 pm (Table 81)	F Fridays only
		S Saturdays only
	E Except Saturdays	¶ By Western National Omnibus (Heavy luggage not conveyed)

Road Services are also operated from Kingsbridge to Thurlestone and Hope

The timetable for the period 17 June to 15 September 1957.

4

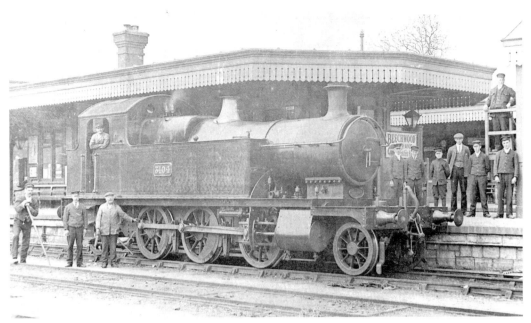

3101 class 2–6–2T No. 3104 stands on the Down loop at Brent. This engine was built in December 1905. Notice that the bridge rail in the foreground has less depth than the bullhead.

c. 1908 Lens of Sutton

55XX class 2–6–2T No. 5558 arriving at Brent with the 11.00 a.m. from Kingsbridge. No. 5558 is in lined green livery.

6.8.58 Hugh Ballantyne

A 'Metro' class 2–4–0T at Avonwick with a Down train. Note the headlamp code and the burnished buffers. The chimney was cropped on the original photograph.

c. 1902 Author's collection

Trains passing at Gara Bridge. The 2–6–2T on the right heads a Down train.

c. 1955 Collection P.Q. Treloar

55XX class 2–6–2T No. 5558 leaving Gara Bridge with the 11.15 a.m. Saturdays-only Kingsbridge–Brent. On the left of the level crossing a poster advertises a day return to Plymouth for 3s 9d.

6.8.60 Hugh Ballantyne

A Down train at Loddiswell. Notice that the canopy stretches right across the wide platform.

c. 1955 Collection P.Q. Treloar

Station staff at Kingsbridge beside a 3101 class 2–6–2T (probably No. 3107) bearing a Wolverhampton works plate.

c. 1906 Lens of Sutton

55XX class 2–6–2T No. 5558, in lined green livery, at Kingsbridge with the 11.00 a.m. to Brent. Notice the corrugated iron carriage shed to the left of the locomotive's smokebox. The engine shed, closed in September 1961, is on the right.

5.8.60 Hugh Ballantyne

Tavistock Junction to Launceston

The Tavistock & South Devon Railway Act was passed on 24 July 1854. The contractors, Messrs Ritson & Blinkhorn, began work on 24 September 1856, and passenger traffic commenced to Tavistock on 22 June 1859, when two special trains covered the 16 miles non-stop in 37 minutes. A goods service began on 1 February 1860. The broad gauge line was leased to the South Devon Railway, which absorbed it on 1 July 1865.

On 30 July 1862 the Launceston & South Devon Railway Act granted powers for an extension from Tavistock. Messrs York & Co. were the contractors and the line opened to passengers on 1 July 1865, an SDR 4-4-0ST hauling the inaugural train of twelve six-wheeled coaches. Goods traffic began on 21 August the same year. The Launceston & South Devon Railway was amalgamated with the SDR on 31 December 1873. A third rail was added between Lydford and Plymouth at a cost of £86,000, to enable the LSWR to run over this section from 17 May 1876, and the branch became part of the LSWR's main line to Plymouth. When the LSWR's own independent line to Plymouth opened on 2 June 1890, the Lydford–Plymouth section reverted to branch status. The remainder of the line was converted to standard gauge between 20 and 23 May 1892.

On 22 September 1943 a chord line was laid at Launceston between the GWR and SR to enable either company to have an alternative route from Plymouth to Cornwall. The Plymouth to Tavistock section of the branch was busy with regular travellers, while up to 20,000 excursionists were carried on bank holidays, but after the Second World War these figures seldom exceeded 2,000. Passenger numbers to and from Tavistock suffered when petrol rationing was abolished in 1950, and in the late '50s winter trains carried fewer than ten passengers, normal trains consisting of a single autotrailer.

The last day of passenger service was Saturday 29 December 1962, but owing to extremely severe weather the last scheduled trains never ran, and the earlier ones had not completed their journey by the end of the day. As a result of the blizzard the last Up train was the 5.40 p.m. Launceston–Plymouth, which arrived at Marsh Mills at 7.50 p.m. It then had to be run into the Down platform, as the Launceston–Plymouth goods train lay abandoned in the correct platform. Frozen points prevented the 5.40 going further, but at 10.05 p.m. it managed to gain the main line by the expedient of splitting the points. Meanwhile, 2-6-2T No. 5568 and four corridor coaches working the 6.20 p.m. Plymouth–Launceston left Plymouth 72 minutes late. It reached Marsh Mills at 10.14 p.m., having covered the 3 miles at an average speed of less than 1¼ mph. Reaching Bickleigh an hour later, it crossed 0-6-0PT No. 6400 and three corridor coaches working the 7.10 p.m. Tavistock South–Plymouth, which had become frozen to the rails, having waited so long to make the crossing.

At Horrabridge passengers on the 6.20 were informed that their train would reach Launceston, though in the event this proved over-optimistic. It actually terminated at Tavistock South on Sunday at 12.23 a.m. As the telegraph wires were down, no staff or ticket could be issued, so the twenty-five passengers spent the night in the first two coaches, warmed by the engine. The signalman and stationmaster loyally remained on duty and provided food. The following day passengers were taken to the church hall and eventually reached home by road.

Three passengers on the 7.10 p.m. from Tavistock South spent the night in Bickleigh signal-box as No. 6400 had run out of water and its fire had to be drawn. The 7.10 was hauled to Plymouth by a relief engine on Sunday afternoon and this was the last passenger-carrying train over the branch. No. 4555 was sent from Plymouth on Monday to help No. 5568 return its train to Plymouth.

On 31 December 1962 goods services were considerably reduced, only continuing to run over the sections from Tavistock Junction to Marsh Mills, Tavistock South to Lydford and Lydford to Lifton (for milk). As traffic from Tavistock South decreased, from 7 September 1964 Lydford–Tavistock South was closed and Lifton to Launceston re-opened. The route from Launceston to Lydford closed completely on 28 February 1966.

The branch left the main line at Tavistock Junction and curved round to Marsh Mills (opened in 1861), where at one time a large flour mill stood adjacent to the Up platform, built in 1894. North of the station were the Dartmoor China Clay Company's workings, which still use rail transport today, while on the other side of the line army sidings were opened on 2 January 1942.

Trains faced an almost unbroken rise at a ruling gradient of 1 in 60 to Yelverton Tunnel. Plym Bridge Platform, a long timber affair later replaced by concrete, opened on 1 May 1906. It was shortened to 100 ft in May 1959. The 130 yd-long Cann Viaduct, constructed of timber on stone piers, as were all those on the line, was replaced by a new structure in blue Staffordshire brick; this was sited very slightly to the east so that it could be built without interference to traffic. In 1890 the 117 yd-long Riverford Viaduct was rebuilt with five rusticated granite arches, while Bickleigh Viaduct, at 159 yd, was rebuilt in 1893 with seven granite arches. A Royal Marine Commando training camp near Bickleigh Station generated traffic. The 171 yd Ham Green Viaduct was rebuilt in 1899 with six arches; this had granite piers but brick arches and parapet.

Shaugh Bridge Platform opened on 19 October 1907 and beyond was Shaugh (or Lee Beer) Tunnel, 307 yd in length with fine granite portals. Clearbrook Halt opened on 29 October 1928, and a young porter with a barrow would wheel cakes from the halt to a local shop. Yelverton station, 500 ft above sea level, was built at the junction with the Princetown branch, but not until 1 May 1885, about two years after the opening of the Princetown line. It had a strange polygonal timber building, and was designed as such because it was sited along the sharply curved branch. A rustic footbridge connected the two parts of Yelverton House gardens, which were severed when the line was built. The station had no goods facilities; instead this traffic was dealt with at Horrabridge. Yelverton Tunnel was absolutely straight and from the platforms daylight was visible at the far end of its 641 yd length. A water tank was provided by the Yelverton portal.

Horrabridge distant signal was near the far end of the tunnel and only a few yards from Yelverton's Up distant signal. For nearly two years Horrabridge acted as the junction of the Princetown branch. Its platforms were set well apart – a legacy of the broad gauge – and the station itself was situated above the village. Beyond the station was Magpie Viaduct, rebuilt as four brick arches in 1900. Walkham (or Grenofen) Viaduct, 367 yd long, was originally regarded, both in engineering and aesthetic terms, as the most perfect example of Brunel's timber viaducts. When rebuilt in 1910, the original piers were raised to rail level to support steel girders. Grenofen Tunnel, 374 yd long, had fine granite horseshoe-shaped portals.

Whitchurch Down Platform opened on 1 September 1906 to serve a suburb of Tavistock. Until 1957 Gas Works Siding was on the west side before Tavistock, which had an imposing train shed. This burnt down in the summer of 1887 when a porter upset a lamp. The shed was rebuilt in the original style but a lesson had been learned: its replacement was in stone, not timber. 'South' was added to its name on 26 September 1949. The station had an extensive goods yard, including a cattle-loading dock. Situated 1½ miles north were sidings serving Pitts Cleave Quarry, but these closed on 7 September 1964. The GWR passed under the LSWR through the short Wringworthy Tunnel. Mary Tavy & Blackdown was an early example of rationalization. After the LSWR opened its independent line to Plymouth, the signal-box and crossing loop at Mary Tavy were taken out of use in 1892. In 1905 the Down platform was used as a poultry run and the elderly stationmaster was reproved for its unkempt appearance. The following year shrubs were planted. The disused platform shelter remained as late as 1959.

The branch now entered the open moor. LSWR and GWR stations at Lydford were adjacent, the GWR being on the west side and a junction provided south of the passenger platforms. The former broad–narrow gauge transfer shed became the goods shed. Unusually, from 8 January 1917 Lydford signal-box had two sets of levers, the GWR frame on the west side and the LSWR's on the east. Lydford, 600 ft above sea level, was at the summit of the line which made a 4 mile descent thereafter at 1 in 77 to Coryton.

Liddaton Halt opened on 4 April 1938 and the next station, Coryton, had only a single platform. At Lifton, sidings served a mill from 1893 until 1966. The Ambrosia Milk Factory opened nearby in 1917, and some of the milk was sent to London in tanks. Milk products were distributed by rail. In 1965 an average of sixteen container loads of rice pudding left daily. Leat Siding, half a mile beyond Lifton, was in use from 1867 to 1942, and the line then crossed into Cornwall over Polson Bridge to end at a terminal station in Launceston.

In standard gauge times 1901 class 0–6–0STs were used, and at the beginning of this century 3521 class 4–4–0s. In 1906 the first of the 45XX class 2–6–2Ts appeared: Nos 2161/5 and Nos 2171/9. 57XX and 64XX class 0–6–0PTs were used and in the 1930s engines of the 'Duke' class appeared on summer Saturdays when traffic was heavy. One summer Saturday in 1931 No. 5013 *Abergavenny Castle* arrived at Yelverton, travelling tender-first with a stopping passenger train from Plymouth. By 1955 the push-pull to Tavistock consisted of an autotrailer and a 14XX 0–4–2T. Early in 1959 45XX class No. 5511, fitted for auto-working, was transferred from Wales to work the branch. After closure to passengers an Okehampton engine, usually a 413XX Ivatt 2–6–2T, worked the freight from Lydford, before a D63XX diesel took over the duty from 1964.

Tavistock had a timber-built engine shed, which opened in June 1859. It closed in 1865, having become redundant when the railway was extended to Launceston, and was re-erected there.

In 1887 the passenger service consisted of five trains each way from Plymouth to Launceston, and the 35½ mile journey took about 105 minutes. On Sundays two trains ran each way and one to Tavistock. The timetable for 1906 showed eleven trains from Plymouth to Tavistock (thirteen on Wednesdays and Saturdays), five of these continuing to Launceston (six on Wednesdays and Saturdays). On Sundays three ran to Launceston, with an extra one to Tavistock only. In 1938 four trains ran through to Launceston with an additional nine to Tavistock, while on Sundays three through trains ran, plus two to Yelverton and three from Yelverton. The cuts of 30 June 1958 saw the withdrawal of the Sunday service. The timetable for the summer of 1961 offered three Down trains to Launceston and an additional three on Saturdays; the journey time was about 95 minutes. An extra five trains operated to Tavistock.

An accident occurred on 18 November 1885 when LSWR Adams 395 class 0–6–0 No. 442 was derailed at 30 mph near Yelverton while working the 4.00 p.m. Exeter–Plymouth passenger train. No. 442 struck a rock face, rebounded across the track and fell down an embankment together with the leading brake van, which became uncoupled. The rest of the train, although derailed, remained upright. The driver was fatally injured, but the fireman, guards and passengers received only cuts and bruises. The Board of Trade inquiry attributed blame to the engine's long (16 ft 6 in) wheelbase and faulty elevation of the curved track. Subsequently this class of engine was banned from working passenger and van trains west of Exeter and restricted to 25 mph on goods services. No. 442, built in 1883, was not withdrawn until 1957.

The Plym Valley Railway
The inaugural meeting of the Plym Valley Railway Association was held on 20 February 1980, and on 27 February 1981 the Plym Valley Railway was incorporated. The latter was responsible for policy, land and rolling stock, while the association provided the workforce. Apart from Bickleigh siding, as the quarter of a mile stub of the branch was known, all track is having to be relaid. From 1991 'The Woodland Line' was added to the PVR's title, as the line is being rebuilt up the wooded valley of the River Plym to Plym Bridge. It is hoped that half a mile of track will be opened in the near future and that Plym Bridge Halt will be reached by about the year 2002.

The stone station at Billacombe on the Yealmpton branch was dismantled and each stone marked. The station is to be re-erected at Marsh Mills, and at the time of writing (November 1994) a start has been made on digging the foundations.

Motive power on the Plym Valley Railway:

Locomotive	Wheel arrangement	Builder	Building date
75079	4–6–0	BR, Swindon	1956
Falmouth Docks No. 3	0–4–0ST	Hawthorn, Leslie	1926
13002, later 08.032	0–6–0D	BR, Derby	1952
Vanguard, ex-Associated Portland Cement, Plymstock	0–4–0DH	Thomas Hill	1963
No. 3281 ex-Coast Lines, Victoria Wharf, Plymouth	0–4–0DM	F.C. Hibberd	1948

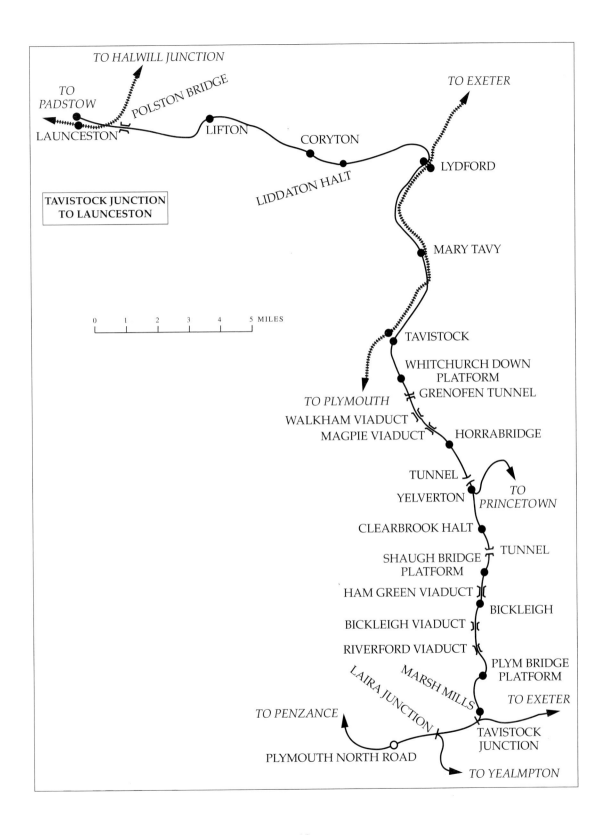

TO HALWILL JUNCTION

TO PADSTOW

POLSTON BRIDGE

LAUNCESTON

LIFTON

CORYTON

LIDDATON HALT

TO EXETER

LYDFORD

**TAVISTOCK JUNCTION
TO LAUNCESTON**

MARY TAVY

0   1   2   3   4   5 MILES

TAVISTOCK

WHITCHURCH DOWN
PLATFORM

GRENOFEN TUNNEL

TO PLYMOUTH

WALKHAM VIADUCT

MAGPIE VIADUCT

HORRABRIDGE

TUNNEL

YELVERTON

TO PRINCETOWN

CLEARBROOK HALT

TUNNEL

SHAUGH BRIDGE
PLATFORM

HAM GREEN VIADUCT

BICKLEIGH

BICKLEIGH VIADUCT

RIVERFORD VIADUCT

PLYM BRIDGE
PLATFORM

LAIRA JUNCTION

MARSH MILLS

TO EXETER

TO PENZANCE

TAVISTOCK
JUNCTION

PLYMOUTH NORTH ROAD

TO YEALMPTON

A 2–6–2T at Marsh Mills with an Up ballast train.

c. 1925 Lens of Sutton

The Plymouth & Dartmoor Railway near Yelverton.

c. 1900 Author's collection

A Down railmotor and trailer at Yelverton, with the Princetown branch curving away to the left.

c. 1910 Author's collection

A 3521 class 4–4–0 enters Yelverton with a Launceston–Plymouth train.

c. 1905 Author's collection

Yelverton, with a train at every platform: 45XX class 2–6–2T No. 4568 has arrived with the 12.08 p.m. from Princetown, 14XX class 0–4–2T No. 1408 is running in with the 12.33 p.m. Tavistock–Plymouth, and 55XX 2–6–2T No. 5567 the 12.12 p.m. Plymouth–Launceston.

20.12.55 Hugh Ballantyne

Adams 0–6–0 No. 442 lies derailed on mixed gauge track (far left) near Yelverton.

18.11.1885 Author's collection

A 3521 class 4–4–0 enters Horrabridge with an Up passenger train. The track is on longitudinal sleepers, while the wide spacing between the roads is a legacy of the broad gauge.

c. 1910 Author's collection

Tavistock station on the opening day of the South Devon & Tavistock Railway.

22.6.1859 Courtesy *Illustrated London News*

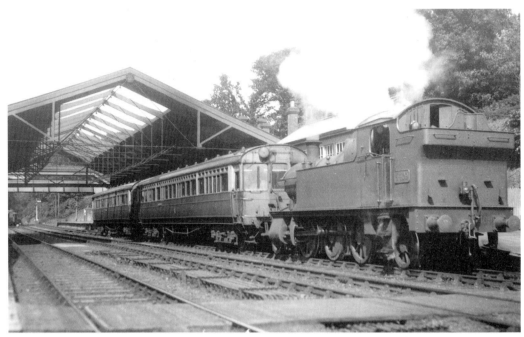

44XX class 2–6–2T No. 4409 at Tavistock with an Up train comprising two autocars.

c. 1948 Lens of Sutton

The disused Down platform at Mary Tavy, which closed in 1892.

c. 1905 Author's collection

The two stations at Lydford: the GWR is the nearer, with the LSWR beyond. An Up GWR train stands at the platform, headed by an 0–6–0 running tender first. The slopes of Black Down are at the top of the picture.

c. 1910 Lens of Sutton

A train hauled by a 2–6–2T arrives at Liddaton Halt, which opened on 4 May 1938.

21.5.51 Author's collection

A goods train stands on the Up line at Lifton. The four vans stand beside the Ambrosia factory. Note the crossing-keeper's cabin beyond the level crossing.

c. 1932 Author's collection

BR Standard class 4MT 4–6–0 No. 75079 at Marsh Mills undergoing restoration before working on the Plym Valley Railway.

18.7.94 Author

Yelverton to Princetown

Thomas Tyrwhitt, later knighted, who improved the town of Dartmouth, had the idea of building a war prison and settlement at Princetown. In 1818 he subscribed £3,000 and collected £27,783 for the construction of the Plymouth & Dartmoor Railway, which was authorized by an Act of 2 July 1819. Built by Hugh McIntosh, the first section opened to King Tor on 26 September 1823. From December 1826 the horse-worked line ran from Princetown stone quarries to wharves at Sutton Pool, Plymouth. In the reverse direction coal, lime and timber were carried. Passengers were very much a subsidiary traffic.

In 1850 Prince Albert visited Tor Royal, Tyrwhitt's home south of Princetown, and proposed that the old prisoner-of-war barracks, then in use as a naphtha factory, be converted for convict use. This suggestion was carried out and a railway, which gave better communication than the tramway, was authorized by Act of 13 August 1878. The contract was let to John MacKay for £22,190. Much of the route followed the tramway, which was purchased for £22,000.

The Princetown Railway opened on 11 August 1883, and as the GWR refused to build a station at the actual junction at Yelverton – it claimed that the cost of one porter was more than the traffic would demand – Horrabridge acted as the junction station until the GWR changed its view and opened a station at Yelverton on 1 May 1885. The GWR was rewarded by Yelverton developing into a holiday resort and dormitory town for Plymouth.

The Princetown Railway was not absorbed into the GWR until 1 January 1922. The branch was susceptible to road competition and closed to passengers and goods on 5 March 1956; the track was lifted the following year. The Princetown branch platform at Yelverton, 500 ft above sea level, was set on a sharp curve and on 22 May 1933 this platform was shortened, allowing the curve to be eased. Before leaving the end of the platform, trains faced a rising gradient of a mile at 1 in 40; 9½ of the 10½ miles were on this gradient. With wet rails and a mixed train, starting could be difficult, and on occasions it took 5 minutes to cover the first quarter of a mile.

Gravity shunting was employed to enable an engine to run round its train – often formed of just a single coach. This was pushed up the branch, the brake applied and the engine run to a siding, after which the guard released the brakes and the coach ran back into the platform. If possible the engine took water at Yelverton in order to avoid using Princetown water, which had to be pumped using steam from the locomotive. Water was so pure that up to eight weeks could be allowed between boiler washouts, whereas at some places this procedure had to be carried out every week or so. The short turntable at Yelverton was used to turn the snowplough.

Beyond Yelverton, black fencing hid trains from horses passing along the Plymouth–Exeter road across Dartmoor, thus preventing the horses being frightened. Dousland passenger station, goods shed and signal-box were made from Roman cement

At Yelverton the fireman of 45XX class 2–6–2T No. 4542 builds his fire ready for the climb. The Princetown branch is to the right and the Tavistock Junction–Launceston line is almost at right angles to the turntable. The point rodding (left) is at right angles to the signal-box (which stands on the left out of the picture). The end of an autocar can be seen protruding beyond the station building.

c. 1956 M.E.J. Deane

of a dismal greenish, greyish-brown tint, the green shade appearing because of vegetable matter in the cement. In 1915 the signal-box by the goods yard was reduced to a ground frame and a new signal-box constructed on the station platform. For many years Dousland was the only intermediate station on the branch. It had no crossing loop.

The track wound round the tors to avoid the expense of making tunnels and embankments on a direct route. It covered 10½ miles to Princetown, yet as the crow flies the distance is less than 6 miles. Burrator Halt, opened on 14 February 1924 as an unadvertised workmen's platform, became public on 18 May 1925. It was officially named Burrator Halt in 1929 and then, at an unknown date, Burrator & Sheepstor. It was in a picturesque situation above Plymouth Corporation's reservoir.

Ingra Tor Halt opened on 2 March 1936. It had a snake warning notice, and a wooden platform like Burrator. Located 1½ miles beyond, sidings serving Swell Tor Quarry were in use from 1883 until 1946. Just over a mile further on were Royal Oak Sidings, serving Foggintor Quarry from 1895 to 1924.

The line spiralled round King Tor for 2½ miles, coming within a quarter of a mile of itself, but 250 ft above the previous level. King Tor Halt, with a platform formed from a sleeper wall backed by earth and topped with gravel, opened on 2 April 1928 to serve quarrymen's cottages. Although classified in timetables as a halt, 'Platform' appeared on the actual nameboard.

Princetown station, goods shed, engine shed and signal-box were of stone rendered with Roman cement. Until about 1930 a corrugated iron shed was provided for the coaches. Timber screens on the passenger platform sheltered travellers from severe winds, Princetown station being the highest in England and 1,372 ft above sea level – only 3 in lower than the highest point in Cornwall. A camping coach was stabled at Princetown from 1934 to 1939. It could be hired for £4 a week as long as its lessees travelled there by rail. Cattle traffic was quite heavy after Princetown cattle fair on the first Wednesday in September. In 1925 the branch despatched forty-four cattle trucks over the whole year. In 1925 Princetown received an average of four coal wagons daily, and two wagons of general goods were forwarded and five received.

When the branch opened in 1883, former Llynvi & Ogmore Railway 0–6–0Ts, GWR Nos 919 and 923, were used. Then 517 class 0–4–2Ts and 19XX class 0–6–0STs worked until the 44XX class 2–6–2Ts appeared in 1905. To ease the engine around curves, in 1931 No. 4402 was fitted with a wheel-flange lubrication system powered by a Westinghouse pump and air reservoir from an ex-ROD 2–8–0. The modification, far from curing the trouble, was found to cause slipping, as did the gravity-feed wheel-flange lubrication system on No. 4407. Nos 4402 and 4410 were then fitted with an apparatus which used steam under pressure to spray coolant on the rails in front of the pony truck on the ascent to Princetown. Two reservoirs alongside the smokebox had to be filled each morning. The apparatus was cleverly designed to feed only the outer rail on a curve and cut off completely on straight track. Lubricators were also fitted to the rear driving wheel flanges to reduce friction on the descent.

Locomotives normally faced Princetown in order to keep the firebox crown covered on the steep gradients of up to 1 in 40. During heavy snowfalls, 1901 class 0–6–0STs fitted with snowploughs ran up and down the branch between trains to clear the snow. Engines of this class were short enough to be turned on the 23 ft 6 in tables at Yelverton and Princetown. There was an engine shed at Princetown, the water tank forming part of its roof, and it was base for two drivers and two firemen. The shed closed in March 1956.

In 1887 five trains ran each way and two on Sundays. Owing to the severe gradients facing Down trains, they were allowed about 32 minutes while Up trains were allowed 29 minutes. In 1910 the timetable showed seven daily services and only one on Sundays, while in 1938 five Down and four Up trains were run on weekdays only. Because halts had been opened, the time allowed was 42 and 38 minutes respectively. Speed was restricted to 20 mph.

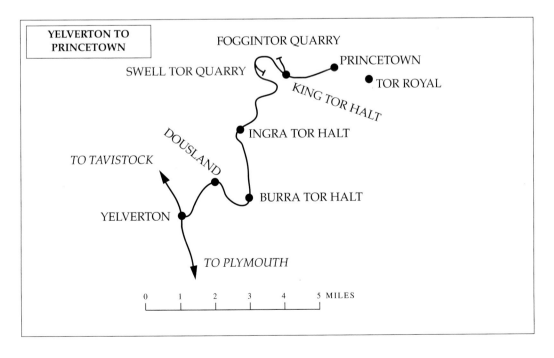

44XX class 2–6–2T No. 4402 having its water tanks filled at Yelverton. Beyond is the Tavistock Junction–Launceston line. Note the brazier near the water crane. This was lit in cold weather to prevent the water from freezing.

c. 1956 M.E.J. Deane

Gravity was used to run the engine around its train. After arrival the engine propelled the coaches up the branch, uncoupled and ran to a siding. The coaches then rolled back to the platform, behind the photographer, and the engine was coupled to them ready for the next trip.

c. 1910 Lens of Sutton

A 44XX class 2–6–2T near Yelverton with a train from Princetown. The 1 in 40 gradient can be appreciated when contrasted with the level siding.

c. 1910 Author's collection

Dousland: a view from the goods shed down towards the passenger station. Both buildings are of Roman cement. The fact that there is no signal-box on the platform indicates that the picture was taken before 1915. In the foreground are the station staff and permanent way men. Note the check rail on the main line.

c. 1910 Lens of Sutton

Burrator and Sheepstor Halt, opened on 18 May 1925, is in a very picturesque setting. Notice how the ground drops away beyond the platform to Plymouth Corporation's reservoir.

c. 1930 Author's collection

A 1901 class 0–6–0ST snowed up on the branch.

c. 1905 Author's collection

Princetown: a view towards Yelverton during the construction of the first three station houses. The goods shed is on the far left.

c. 1905 Lens of Sutton

The three station houses at Princetown have been completed in this view. W. Bolt's coal-storage shed is in the centre right, while to the left is the signal-box of unusual design. The nearest wagon contains loco coal.

c. 1910 Author's collection

45XX class 2–6–2T No. 4542, having arrived at Princetown with a mixed train, has uncoupled from the corridor coach. To the left is the goods shed and hand crane.

c. 1956 M.E.J. Deane

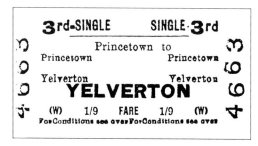

A Princetown to Yelverton ticket.

The Yealmpton Branch

The Plymouth & Dartmoor Railway Act of 28 June 1888 authorized the South Hams Railway to run from Plymstock on the Turnchapel branch to Modbury, but before it could be built the GWR promoted a more direct line to Yealmpton. To avoid costly competition the GWR agreed to modify its proposal and reroute the branch via the LSWR's Plymstock line. The opening of the LSWR extension to Turnchapel entitled that company to running powers over the GWR to Yealmpton, as the LSWR intended continuing the line on to Modbury. The Plymouth & Dartmoor Railway Act of 17 August 1894 transferred to the GWR powers to build the Yealmpton Railway, but the LSWR lost interest in the proposed Modbury extension. John Aird won the contract for building the line to Yealmpton.

The Yealmpton Railway opened to passengers on 17 January 1898 and to goods the following day. The branch was isolated from the rest of the GWR as its only access was over LSWR metals. As a result of competition from buses, the branch closed to passengers as early as 7 July 1930, only to re-open on 21 July 1941 during the Second World War to provide transport for Plymouth residents who were living in the country, either to avoid bombing, or because their homes had been destroyed. At first only a workmen's service was provided, but the branch was opened to the public on 3 November 1941. Eventually it closed to passengers on 7 October 1947, although goods continued until 29 February 1960.

Yealmpton trains started from Plymouth Millbay, joining the LSWR at Cattewater Junction before crossing Laira Viaduct parallel with the A379 road bridge. Plymstock station, constructed of timber and corrugated iron, had two platforms in a V-shape, the Turnchapel and Yealmpton lines both being single. An economy was made on 14 July 1935 when the signal-box was closed and a new lever frame placed in the ticket office. The office was bombed in 1941 and a new frame was installed on 12 October the same year.

Billacombe, like all the branch stations, had a single platform. The station building there, and at Brixton Road and Yealmpton, was of standard GWR design, but executed in stone instead of red brick. The sidings, serving a goods shed, were worked from a ground frame.

The gradient rose to Elburton Cross, which had just a platform with a simple timber building and no goods sidings. The line fell to Brixton Road, where the signal-box closed around 1925 and was replaced by two ground frames. Steer Point had simple timber buildings on its platform. Between 1901 and 1959 a private siding served the adjacent brickworks. At Steer Point the branch came alongside the Yealm estuary and then followed it to Yealmpton.

The passenger platform at Yealmpton was quite long. The station itself had a fairly extensive goods yard, designed as a through rather than a terminal layout, as the original concept was for the line to be extended to Modbury. As the sidings faced east, the headshunt was at that end of the yard. In 1925 a daily average of eight coal wagons were received; seven general goods wagons were forwarded and three received; 103 cattle trucks and 3,352 milk churns were dealt with annually. The signal-box closed on 23 January 1931 and was replaced by three ground frames.

The 1910 timetable offered quite a good service of nine trains each way daily and three on Sundays, taking 36 minutes from Plymouth Millbay to Yealmpton. Speed on the branch was limited to 30 mph.

Trains were generally worked by tank engines, but in the early years of this century steam railmotors appeared. For the final months of its existence as a goods-only branch, 112XX class diesels were used.

Although the railway itself never reached Modbury, the first GWR bus service near Plymouth ran between Yealmpton and Modbury. It started on 2 May 1904, the GWR having taken it over from a private company.

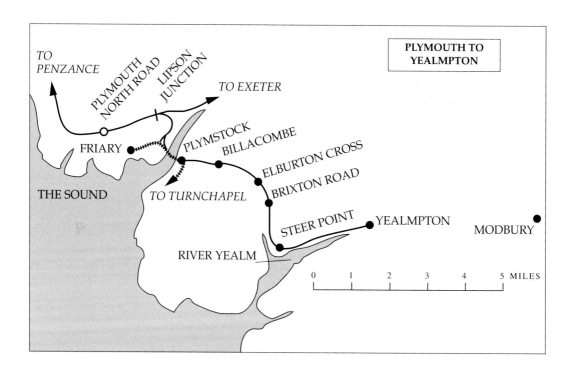

An 0–6–0ST enters Plymstock with a train from Yealmpton. The line on the right is the LSWR branch to Turnchapel. The station building consists of timber and corrugated iron. Note the 'barley sugar stick' lamp-posts.

c. 1910 Author's collection

Drewry diesel-mechanical 204 b.h.p. 0–6–0 No. 2229 shunting at Plymstock. Note the gradient post beneath the station nameboard.

c. 1962 Lens of Sutton

8750 class 0–6–0PT No. 9716 at Billacombe shunting the 10.40 a.m. Laira Yard–Yealmpton.
17.3.58 Hugh Davies

8750 class 0–6–0PT No. 9716 at Brixton Road with the 10.40 a.m. Laira Yard–Yealmpton.
17.3.58 Hugh Davies

A steam railmotor pushing a trailer to Yealmpton leaves Steer Point on the Yealm estuary.

c. 1910 Lens of Sutton

At Yealmpton an 0–6–0ST hauls a stopping train to Plymouth. The square spigot lamp fixing, rather than a bracket, suggests that the photograph was taken before 1903.

c. 1902 Author's collection

A steam railcar from Plymouth arrives at Yealmpton.

c. 1912 Author's collection

Yealmpton, looking towards Plymouth. An RCTS special comprises autocars W193W, W225W, 64XX class 0–6–0PT No. 6420 and autocars W189W and W229W.

2.5.59 Hugh Ballantyne

The Millbay Docks Branch

The GWR, Bristol & Exeter Railway and the South Devon Railway were allies of the Plymouth Great Western Dock Company, incorporated on 18 August 1846 to construct Millbay Docks and a rail connection which opened early in 1850. The following year saw the inauguration of a monthly steamer service from Plymouth to India, Australia and China. An Act of 1874 enabled the associated companies (GWR, B&ER and SDR) to acquire the dock company. On 18 June 1878 the docks branch was converted to mixed gauge, standard gauge trucks being worked from North Road by broad gauge engines.

As demand for speedier world communications increased, the GWR took off mails from ocean liners at Plymouth and rushed them to Bristol and Paddington, while passengers remained on board ship until it docked at Southampton. From 1893 passengers were taken off too.

Plymouth developed as an important port of arrival from Australia and India and had a very large share of the American mails and passengers. Liners, often bound for the Continent, arrived at Cawsand Bay at the south end of Plymouth Sound, and only came inside the breakwater in very stormy weather. No time was wasted; two GWR tenders were secured one on each side, and 30 minutes later the transfer was complete and the liner continued on her voyage.

During the summer months three American liners called weekly, each transferring 100–150 passengers and 400–500 mail bags. The special passenger trains varied in length between four and twelve bogie vehicles, comprising coaches, dining-car, mail vans and bullion van. At first specials were run for each liner and on at least one occasion a solitary passenger landed by tender and demanded a special, but by 1904 economics demanded a minimum of twenty-five first class passengers, or their equivalent in mixed classes. Passengers using the specials enjoyed reduced fares. In 1904 ocean rates for Millbay–Paddington were: first class, £1 10s; second class, 18s 9d; third class, 15s. An additional charge of 2s 6d per passenger was made to cover landing and dock charges.

The docks comprised an outer harbour of about 30 acres and an inner basin of approximately 13 acres. Tenders moored at a pier in the outer harbour. An Ocean Special stood on the quay in two sections: the inner half consisted of passenger coaches and the outer half of mail, baggage and bullion vans. Immediately one section was loaded, the two halves were shunted together and coupled. Prompt despatch was the keyword – the 30 minutes from the arrival of the tenders to the departure of the train was sufficient to cover transfer and customs formalities. Passengers were landed at the open wharf until 1905, when the chief engineer, J.C. Inglis, had it covered. Facilities included a waiting room with booking office.

Disappointed with the number of passengers compared with the number of coaches on an Ocean Special, G. Grant, Divisional Superintendent, Plymouth, investigated the problem. His report read: 'Porters were puzzled to find seats. They saw the four corners of a compartment occupied by rugs, bags and paraphernalia, concluding there were as many passengers.' But this was not always so. Grant solved the problem thus: 'All compartments were lettered, seats numbered and passengers required to purchase a voucher before being given a numbered seat, and the trouble ceased.'

At first the Ocean Mail trains stopped at Bristol to transfer bags for the north of England, but later a slip coach was used. To utilize the tenders more fully, when not occupied with visiting liners, excursion trips were run to Eddystone lighthouse.

The LSWR also operated a service to meet liners and in 1910, to abolish cut-throat competition, the LSWR ended its shipping activities at Plymouth, while the GWR withdrew its Plymouth–Brest ferry. In the 1920s an electrically powered conveyor belt was installed to transfer mails from tender to train. The best year for the GWR Ocean Specials was 1930, when 45,300 passengers were carried.

The 1936 improvements to the docks station included a new reception hall with seats for 170 passengers, buffet, facilities for the despatch of cables and telegrams, and a money exchange. The floor was covered with Korkoid bearing a bright and attractive pattern. 'Land at Plymouth and Save a Day' was the slogan.

In the late 1930s Plymouth dealt with an average of 500 liners annually, landing 30,000–40,000 passengers. In 1937 the *Queen Mary* called nine times and the *Normandie* four. When the *Queen Mary* made her first call on 15 March 1937 four tenders went alongside. Two special trains were run to Paddington; one weighing 326 tons took 3 hours 51 minutes and the other, weighing 412 tons, took 4 hours 5 minutes, including stopping at Newton Abbot to uncouple the assisting engine. These trains carried many celebrities, including such film stars as Douglas Fairbanks Jr, Mary Pickford and Richard Dix.

In 1946 646 Australian brides of British servicemen were landed and on 14 December 1946 no fewer than 27,000 mail bags arrived from an American ship – the largest number ever handled at Plymouth. In 1952 new accommodation was opened for ocean passengers and in 1957 19,203 passengers were carried and 40,739 mail bags landed. Tens of thousands of West Indians arrived at Plymouth during the 1950s.

In November 1961 French Line vessels ceased using Plymouth and one of the two tenders was withdrawn. Complete boat trains were discontinued, although for a few months passengers travelled in coaches added to ordinary service trains. Tracks south of Millbay Crossing signal-box were transferred from BR to the British Transport Docks Board in 1963. All rail traffic at the docks was withdrawn on 30 June 1971 and the branch closed.

Plymouth Dock had a single road, stone-walled locomotive shed, opened by the SDR in around 1869. Generally two 0–6–0STs were stabled there. It closed in about 1955.

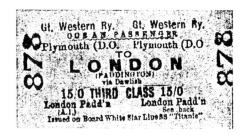

A third-class ocean passenger ticket for Millbay–Paddington. This was intended to be issued on board the SS *Titanic*.

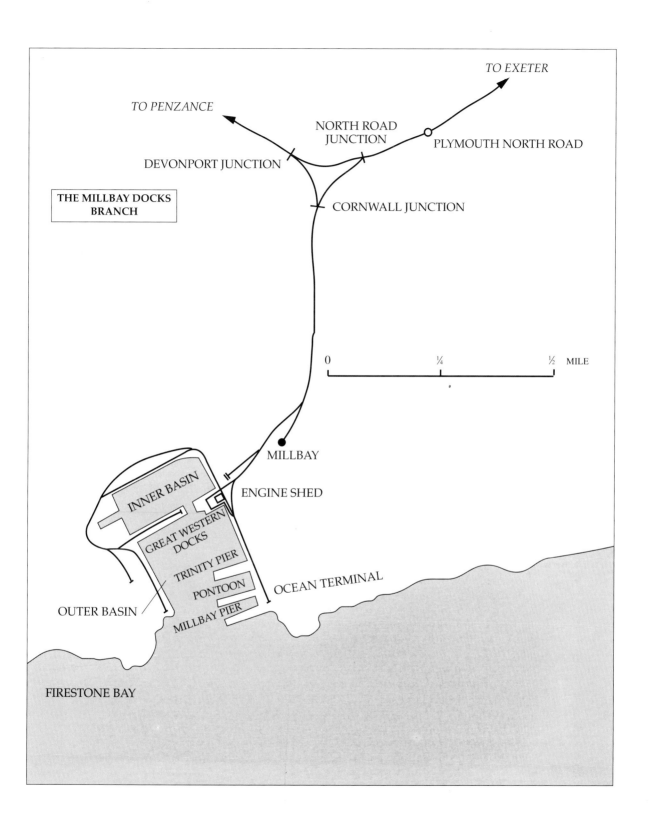

TO EXETER

TO PENZANCE

NORTH ROAD
JUNCTION

PLYMOUTH NORTH ROAD

DEVONPORT JUNCTION

**THE MILLBAY DOCKS
BRANCH**

CORNWALL JUNCTION

0   ¼   ½   MILE

MILLBAY

INNER BASIN

ENGINE SHED

GREAT WESTERN
DOCKS

TRINITY PIER

OCEAN TERMINAL

PONTOON

OUTER BASIN

MILLBAY PIER

FIRESTONE BAY

Plymouth Millbay gauge conversion taking place at 6.00 p.m. on a Saturday.

21.5.1892 Author's collection

The first Up standard gauge train leaves Plymouth Millbay at 8.35 a.m., headed by a 3521 class 0–4–4T. The goods shed is on the right and on the left is the narrow ticket platform.

23.5.1892 Author's collection

An Ocean Special headed by a 4–4–0 passes the upper end of Millbay yard.

c. 1903 Author's collection

A two-coach Ocean Special leaves Millbay Docks station, headed by an 0–6–0ST.

c. 1906 Author's collection

The waiting room at Millbay Docks station for passengers from ocean liners.

c. 1903 Author's collection

Millbay Docks. Transferring the mail was expensive in terms of labour. A line of men can be seen carrying sacks to the Post Office stowage vans (centre left). The ocean liner tender, with mail bags stacked in its bows, is in the foreground.

c. 1903 Author's collection

At Millbay Docks a conveyor tips mailbags into Post Office stowage van No. 823, built in 1904.

c. 1935 GWR

Millbay Docks. *Sir John Hawkins* was a tender for carrying passengers and mail from liners.

c. 1935 GWR

Broad gauge ex-Torbay & Brixham Railway 0–4–0ST No. 2175 *Raven*, which shunted at Millbay Docks. Note the spark arrester on the chimney. In August 1892 the locomotive was converted to standard gauge and renumbered 1329. It was sold to the Wantage Tramway in 1910.

c. 1892 Author's collection

1361 class 0–6–0ST No. 1364 at Millbay Docks.

26.7.48 Collection P.Q. Treloar

Venn Cross to Barnstaple

The Devon & Somerset Railway, a line promoted by landowners between Norton Fitzwarren and Barnstaple, received its Act on 29 July 1864. The same year the contractor started work at Barnstaple, but was almost immediately replaced by another. Owing to a lack of investment, the new contractors, Messrs Pickering, ceased work between September 1866 and May 1870, when the contract was given to John Langham Reed. On 8 June 1871 the branch opened from Norton Junction (as Norton Fitzwarren was then called) to Wiveliscombe.

In 1872 Richard Hassard, the DSR engineer, had a conversation with Henry Ellis, a B&ER director, about the gauge of the line. If the DSR directors had realized the full import of this conversation they could have saved the thousands of pounds which the gauge conversion cost. Ellis stated that the opinion of his board had greatly changed regarding the broad gauge, and that if the DSR approached the B&ER directors it might be possible to change the gauge. Unfortunately the DSR directors ignored this hint and continued laying the more expensive broad gauge, only to be told 2½ years later that the B&ER had resolved to convert its lines to standard gauge. This, of course, meant that the DSR had to follow suit.

Meanwhile, work on the line between Wiveliscombe and Barnstaple had been proceeding. It opened on 1 November 1873 and from 1 August 1876 the B&ER was amalgamated with the GWR, so the latter took over working the DSR. On 16 September 1880 the agreement with the GWR was sealed for narrowing the gauge. Platelayers were brought in from other districts to assist with the conversion, which took place between 15 and 17 May 1881, the last broad gauge train running over the line on Saturday 14 May. A standard gauge goods train and two passenger trains ran on 18 May, the full service operating from the following day.

Ordinary shareholders saw that their line would never make a profit and sold it to the GWR on 1 July 1901. Although busy during the Second World War, afterwards the increase in road transport meant that the branch became uneconomic, and it closed on 1 October 1966, except for the section from Barnstaple Junction to Victoria Road. This was worked as a goods siding until its closure on 5 March 1970.

Venn Cross station was literally on the border between Devon and Somerset, the boundary passing between the signal-box and goods shed. Situated in a cutting 666 ft above sea level, the station was in one of the worst situations for drifting snow. Its design was unusual for the West Country in thatiit had its offices at the top of the cutting instead of by the platform. In 1930 2,023 tickets were sold. Beyond the station the line fell at 1 in 60 to the crossing loop at Morebath station. Here 1,668 tickets were sold in 1930. The line undulated to Morebath Junction, where the Exe Valley branch joined (see *Branch Lines of Devon: Exeter and South, Central and East Devon*). Beyond was Morebath Junction Halt, which opened on 1 December 1928 and whose single platform was only long enough to hold one coach. As the approach to it could be muddy, it was the custom for passengers to leave their Wellington boots under the waiting-shed seat and change into shoes for the train journey.

B.R. 4452

British Transport Commission (W) EXCESS FARE TICKET

ISSUED AT ... TAUNTON UP L/ 45681

Train............ Date.............. (month in words)

Ticket held No........ Description............
From........ To........
EXCESSED FROM........
TO........
VIA........
(For alternative routes see book of routes)

Cause & Description of Excess	Class	No. of Passengers (in words)		Amount		
		Single	Return	£	s.	d.
Without tickets Description:—						
Short of destination						
Out of date						
Difference between						
Second to First						

Valid until........................ Collected by........................
Issued subject to the Regulations and Conditions in the Commission's Publications and Notices applicable to British Railways.
NOT TRANSFERABLE

An excess-fare ticket for Morebath–Taunton.

2.8.66

The line crossed the River Exe and temporarily returned to Somerset. It regained Devon as it entered East Anstey station, 700 ft above sea level and the highest point on the branch. It sold 4,297 tickets in 1930. Unlike many branch stations, coal traffic was light, with an average of only about three trucks a year, as fuel used in the area was predominantly wood. Rabbits were an important traffic before myxomatosis. Following the monthly cattle market adjacent to the station, one or two cattle trucks were despatched. The cattle pens had to be hosed down, the signalman working the handpump in the gentlemen's lavatory while the lad porter scraped away at the cowpats, as the water pressure was insufficient to do the job effectively.

Yeo Mill Halt, with a timber-built platform one coach long, opened on 27 June 1932. Almost 3½ miles beyond was Bishop's Nympton & Molland (known simply as Molland until 1 March 1876), which issued 5,084 tickets in 1930. Because of the ground slope, the Up platform had to be supported on arches of blue brick. About 3 miles further on, and half a mile east of South Molton, was a trailing exchange siding with the Florence Mining Company's tramway, the ironstone being carried to Bridgwater. From 2 May 1928 the Down road at South Molton was signalled for two-way working and unless two trains were required to cross, the Down platform was also used by Up trains, as this platform could be most conveniently reached by road. In 1930 12,132 tickets were sold. The goods yard dealt with 600–700 wagons monthly and was the starting point seasonally of a daily rabbit special consisting of two parcels vans and sometimes a horse-box. The line then passed through the 321 yd Castle Hill Tunnel and beyond crossed the Bray Valley on a six-span wrought-iron lattice-girder viaduct 232 yd long and 94 ft high. It contained 7,000 tons of masonry and 400 tons of iron.

```
No. 897
        GREAT  WESTERN  RAILWAY.
         TRAIN  STAFF  TICKET.
        BARNSTAPLE.
                                (DOWN.)
Train No._____
    To the Engine-driver.
        You are authorised, after seeing the Train Staff
    for the Section, to proceed from BARNSTAPLE SOUTH
    JUNCTION   to   BARNSTAPLE   JUNCTION,   SOUTHERN
    RLY., and the Train Staff will follow.
            Signature of Person in Charge_____
    Date_____
```

A train staff ticket, coloured blue, which was issued to a driver at Barnstaple South Junction for Barnstaple Junction, SR, when another train was following. It prevented the staff from being at the wrong end of the line.

Date unknown Collection W.G. Crook

Filleigh station (known as Castle Hill until 1 January 1881) had a Down platform, which was added on 7 May 1937. The station was used by pupils and staff of West Buckland School and dealt with their luggage. A total of 5,752 tickets were sold in 1930. A GWR lorry from Filleigh delivered to Parracombe and Lynton, which meant that consignees were saved the trouble of collecting items. In contrast, the Lynton & Barnstaple Railway failed to deliver from stations and this was one reason for its closure.

The architecture of Swimbridge station differed from the others on the branch. The stone building on the Down platform was quite small and the brick and timber waiting shelter on the Up was more weatherproof than the others. A total of 5,574 tickets were sold in 1930. Between ten and twelve cattle trucks for Banbury were loaded on Tuesdays and Fridays, and the tanyard received skins from Liverpool.

West of Swimbridge the moorland changed to flatter countryside before reaching the Barnstaple, Victoria Road, terminus, which was constructed of timber. It had a long platform to cater with train arrivals, and a shorter bay was adequate for departures. The number of tickets sold in 1930 was 20,423. Five or six GWR lorries were kept busy collecting and delivering goods. However, the station closed to passenger traffic on 13 June 1960.

An Act of 31 July 1885 authorized a connecting line between Victoria Road and the LSWR at Barnstaple Junction. This link opened on 1 June 1887 and allowed the GWR to run through trains to Ilfracombe. At South Loop Junction signal-box it joined a curve, opened on 1 July 1905, which formed the third side of a triangular junction and avoided a reversal at Victoria Road. The curve was generally open from July to

45

September, when it was used by holiday trains. The curve closed on 4 September 1939, but re-opened on 13 June 1960, when Victoria Road closed to passengers. The line crossed the River Taw by a five-span girder bridge and joined the LSWR just south of Barnstaple Junction.

From its opening the line was worked by B&ER broad gauge 0–6–0s, 0–6–0STs and 4–4–0STs. After it was narrowed, GWR 2–4–0s, 4–4–0s, 0–6–0s and 2–4–0Ts were used. Around 1925 43XX class 2–6–0s appeared and handled most of the traffic, but their steps had to be cut to a width of 8 ft 4 in to give sufficient clearance when working over the SR's Ilfracombe line. With the introduction of diesel power in the autumn of 1964, trains were generally composed of DMUs varying from one to three cars in length.

A two-road, timber-built engine shed was provided at Barnstaple, Victoria Road. Its short turntable had been transferred from Wiveliscombe when that station ceased to be the terminus and the line was extended. The table was only long enough for a tank engine, and tender locomotives had to turn on the triangle (if it was open), or use the SR table at Barnstaple Junction.

When the branch opened six trains ran each way daily. The summer of 1923 saw nine trains each way, of which four Down only stopped at principal stations. Even in 1966 six trains ran each way daily and nine on Saturdays. Although the GWR marked the branch on its maps as a main line, it really had the character of a branch.

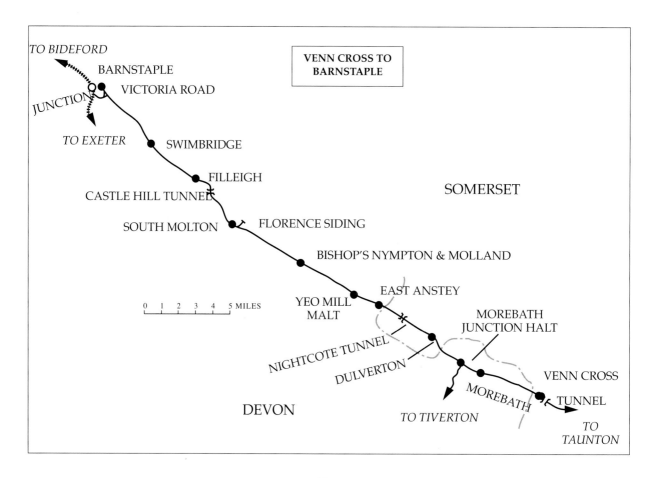

A derailment west of Venn Cross, when wagons ran away.

May 1948 J. Elson

43XX class 2–6–0 No. 7304 (of 83B, Taunton) with an SR coach set at East Anstey.

c. 1958 M.E.J. Deane

An 0–6–0 heading a Down broad gauge passenger train at South Molton. Note the signal-box on stilts. This was replaced around 1901 by a standard building on the Down platform.

1874 Author's collection

A broad gauge 0–6–0ST heading a Down goods at South Molton. Note the timber retaining the platform.

1874 Author's collection

An oil lamp at Filleigh station.
c. 1936 Author's collection

Castle Hill Viaduct, Filleigh.

c. 1873 Author's collection

'Bulldog' class 4–4–0 No. 3416 *John W. Wilson* in the snow at Swimbridge. The train is from Taunton to Barnstaple. The 'B' headlamp is in an unorthodox lower position on the buffer beam.

c. 1930 D.E.H. Box

Between Swimbridge and Barnstaple the coupling of the 12.45 p.m. Taunton–Barnstaple goods train snapped. Later the two halves of the train collided. The damaged wagons were chained together and moved to a siding, where this picture was taken.

c. 1953 W.G. Crook

A 43XX class 2–6–0 passing Acland Cross with a Down passenger train comprised of a motley assortment of coaching stock. The two elliptical-roofed coaches at the rear, one roof-boarded, are evidently a through portion to Ilfracombe. This is confirmed by the position of the horse-box behind the engine, to avoid a shunt at Barnstaple, Victoria Road.

c. 1928 A. Halls

G. W. RLY.   S.3
The holder is prohibited from
entering the Company's Trains

Not Transferable
ADMIT ONE to PLATFORM   1 D
Available ONE HOUR on DAY of
ISSUE ONLY
This Ticket must be given up on
leaving Platform
FOR CONDITIONS SEE BACK

BARNSTAPLE
G. W.

9655   9655

A Barnstaple platform ticket.

A 3521 class 4–4–0 leaves Barnstaple, Victoria Road, for Taunton. The train consists of a bogie coach and a close-coupled set of four four-wheeled coaches.

c. 1925 Collection R.T. Clement

'Bulldog' class 4–4–0 No. 3348 *Launceston* at Barnstaple, Victoria Road. The fireman has uncoupled the engine and removed the headlamp. Notice that the station is built of timber.

Spring 1926 A. Halls

Barnstaple, Victoria Road, station, viewed from the buffer stops. A Dean Standard Goods 0–6–0 has arrived tender first with a passenger train from Barnstaple Junction. At the buffer stops it will run round, to leave for Taunton chimney first. In the centre right is a gas cylinder wagon for recharging coaches and the restaurant car, while on the far right are cattle wagons with coaches in front. Note the variety of advertisements on the fence and building.

c. 1912 Lens of Sutton

A ticket for the last train over the branch. Notice that what appears to be the ticket number is actually the dates of the opening and closing years.

1966 Author's collection

Plymouth, Friary to Turnchapel

The Plymouth & Dartmoor Railway Act of 2 August 1883 authorized a line from Laira to Turnchapel. It opened as far as Pomphlett for goods traffic only on 25 June 1888 and to passengers on 5 September 1892 (when Pomphlett station was renamed Plymstock, even though this was a mile distant).

Meanwhile, on 3 July 1891 the Plymouth & Dartmoor Railway Act revised powers for a line to Turnchapel. Relf & Pethick carried out the contract for constructing the branch, and Lapthorne & Gould of Plymouth were responsible for Hooe Lake Bridge.

Making the Board of Trade inspection in May 1896, Lt.-Col. Addison failed the line, as the Hooe Lake swing bridge arrangements 'did not appear to be sufficient to ensure safety, as the bridge can be opened whilst a train is on the line approaching it'. It was subsequently modified so that when the bridge opened a circuit was broken and the single line electric tablet could not be issued. Similarly, when a tablet was withdrawn the bridge could not be opened. The Plymstock branch was extended to Turnchapel on 1 January 1897 and was worked by the LSWR.

As Turnchapel's attractive beach was within a few minutes' walk of the station, a large number of trippers used the branch. A railmotor service, the first on the LSWR in the south-west, was inaugurated on 10 October 1904, but the vehicles did not prove a success and were replaced by a locomotive-worked push–pull train of two 'gated stock' carriages on which tickets were economically issued and collected by a travelling conductor. By 1934 the conductor had been dispensed with and a junior porter travelled on the train between Lucas Terrace Halt and Turnchapel to issue and collect tickets and act as porter at stations where no staff were on duty. He would indicate to the driver when the platform work was completed. When working an Up push–pull without a guard, 100 yd from the Cattewater Junction Up Home signal, the driver in the control compartment leading the train, as a safety measure, was required to give his fireman, on the engine at the rear, two rings on the bell signal. In the absence of this sound from the driver, the fireman had to be prepared to stop the train.

On Saturdays and at holiday periods, the branch train was strengthened by up to six vehicles, in which case the engine had to run around at the end of each trip, unless a turnover engine was provided. Owing to a fuel crisis, the branch temporarily closed to passengers from January to 2 July 1951 and permanently on 10 September 1951. It was an unusual branch in that its main competitor was the ferry rather than the motor bus, as steamers had to travel only half the distance. The line south of Plymstock closed to freight on 2 October 1961 and today even the service to Plymstock has been withdrawn.

Trains started from the four-platformed Plymouth, Friary terminus, and at Friary 'A' signal-box they crossed the Down main to a single-track branch. This ran parallel to Lucas Terrace Halt, which opened in October 1905 and was extended at its western end in 1923. Both platform and waiting shelter were made of concrete. Beyond, the line curved to cross the GWR's Sutton Harbour branch. It then passed over Laira Viaduct and arrived at Plymstock; Turnchapel trains curved to use the right-hand platform. At one time this station enjoyed a service of over sixty LSWR and GWR trains daily. After closure to passenger traffic, the station site continued to be used for sidings to a cement works and the South Western Gas Board.

Oreston had a small timber-built waiting room and behind the platform was a private siding. Approaching Turnchapel was Bayly's Wharf ground frame, where a siding curved left and passed under the branch before terminating at timber sidings. The branch crossed the 94 yd-long Hooe Lake swing bridge to Turnchapel, the LSWR's southernmost station. The single platform had a timber waiting shelter. A run-round loop was provided. Adjacent quarry sidings, opened in March 1927, were taken over for Air Ministry use in 1944. Beyond the platform a line passed through a tunnel and terminated at the Admiralty's Turnchapel Quay, which comprised an oil depot and other facilities.

T1 class 0–4–4Ts and B4 class 0–4–0Ts worked goods trains. The latter had spark arresters to enable them to shunt the timber yard at Oreston. Because of the gradients, the B4s were limited to twelve loaded wagons and a brake van. O2 class 0–4–4Ts worked passenger trains, though in the early 1930s an ex-LBSCR D1 class 0–4–2T was tried, but it did not prove a success.

The opening service of seven trains to Pomphlett in 1892 had increased by 1910 to twenty-one trains to Turnchapel. No trains ran on Sundays in 1910, but by 1938 the service had improved to twenty-seven trains on weekdays and no fewer than seventeen on Sundays. The 2½ mile journey took 10 minutes.

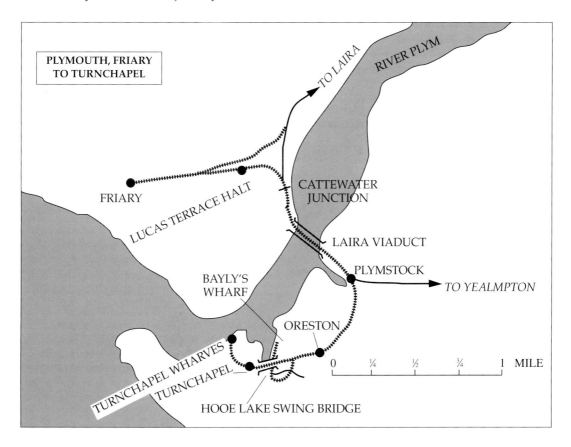

Plymouth Friary, looking towards the buffers. There are two tank engines present (centre), and a 4–4–0 heads the train on the right. The goods shed stands on the left.

c. 1910 Lens of Sutton

Lucas Terrace Halt, photographed after its closure to passengers. The view is to the west of Friary locomotive shed.

c. 1955 Lens of Sutton

H12 class railmotor No. 2 on the Turnchapel service. A board bearing its destination can be seen below the eaves. Note the solid wheels outside the bogie frames and the lattice gate.

October 1904 Author's collection

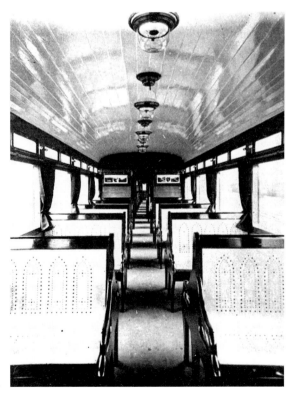

The interior of an H12 class steam railcar.
1904 Author's collection

An H12 class railcar at Turnchapel. The view is looking towards Plymouth.

c. 1905 Author's collection

A two-coach train from Friary at Turnchapel, headed by O2 class 0–4–4T No. 182. The compressed air cylinders on the running plate show that it has been fitted with motor train equipment for push-pull working. Note the disc and tail lamp.

c. 1933 Lens of Sutton

The Cattewater, Friary, Stonehouse Pool and Sutton Harbour Branches

On 2 July 1821 the Plymouth & Dartmoor Railway Act authorized an extension of its tramway from Laira to Cattedown and Sutton Pool. A broad gauge rail was added to the PDR's 4 ft 6 in gauge in May 1853, still for horse traction, and the line was rebuilt for locomotive working between 1856 and 1857, though in the event this did not start until 19 April 1869. One of the wooden sheds which had formed a temporary terminus at Laira was converted into a goods shed for use at Sutton Harbour. The Sutton Harbour Improvement Act of 18 July 1872 allowed the mixed gauge railway to be extended to the north and west sides of the pool.

An Act of 19 July 1875 allowed the LSWR to build its Friary branch, and this opened on 1 February 1878. An Act of the same date authorized the PDR to build its Cattewater branch, which was worked by the LSWR and eventually, by an Act of 16 August 1909, was purchased by that company. Meanwhile, the LSWR had opened its Friary and Sutton Harbour branch on 22 October 1879, the GWR opening its line to North Quay on 6 November 1879.

As an economy following nationalization, the line from Friary to Sutton Harbour closed in November 1950, the only access from then on being via the former GWR's North Quay branch. The GWR's Sutton Harbour branch had been converted to standard gauge between 20 and 23 May 1892. The North Quay branch closed in 1969, the ex-GWR's Sutton Harbour goods depot closed on 31 December 1973 and the site of the track from Friary Junction was largely incorporated in a new road, Gdynia Way, named after Plymouth's twin town in Poland.

Friary marshalling yard gained importance following the closure of Tavistock Junction yard on 4 January 1971. However, Friary was subsequently closed, the track cut back to the station throat and a run-round loop formed for traffic reversing onto the Cattewater branch. Cattewater Junction, just north of Laira Viaduct, was where the single line to Plymstock and Cattewater divided. At a distance of 1¼ miles from Laira Junction the line passed through the 48 yd Cattedown Tunnel. The branch served numerous industries including a quarry and cement works, Dukes Dock and Victoria Pier; the headshunt was in a 30 yd-long terminal tunnel. Today only the Esso bitumen sidings are in use, and one or two trains run daily Mondays to Fridays. Three B4 class 0-4-0Ts shunted at Cattewater, and between Cattewater and Friary trains were limited to thirty loaded wagons and a brake van.

The LSWR's single-track branch to Sutton Harbour curved away southwards just east of Friary station. It then entered a cutting and tunnel, emerging to pass over Sutton Road level crossing; near North Quay it made a junction with the GWR.

STONEHOUSE POOL BRANCH.

DOWN TRAINS—WEEK DAYS.

Distance from Devonport. M. C.		1 Goods. arr.	dep.	2 Goods. arr.	dep.	3 Goods. arr.	dep.
		a.m.	a.m.	p.m.	noon	p.m.	p.m.
...	Devonport	...	8 45	...	12 0	...	5 0
1 23	Stonehouse Pool	8 50	...	12 5	...	5 5	...

UP TRAINS—WEEK DAYS.

Distance from Stonehouse Pool. M. C.		1 Goods. arr.	dep.	2 Goods. arr.	dep.	3 Goods. arr.	dep.
		a.m.	a.m.	p.m.	p.m.	p.m.	p.m.
...	Stonehouse Pool	...	9 5	...	12 20	...	5 20
23	Devonport	9 10	...	12 25	...	5 25	...

The above Trains will run when required and as ordered by Devonport
The load of Trains from Stonehouse Pool to Devonport must be limited to 9 Wagons and 1 Van, which must be at the Rear.

FRIARY AND SUTTON HARBOUR BRANCH.

DOWN TRAINS—WEEK DAYS.

Dist. M. C.	STATIONS.	1 Goods. arr.	dep.	2 Goods. arr.	dep.
		a.m.	a.m.	p.m.	p.m.
...	Friary	...	8 30	...	6 15
1 2	Sutton Harbour	8 35	...	6 20	...

The load of Trains from Friary to Sutton Harbour must be limited to 8 Wagons and 1 Van. Trains must not leave Friary until the Lines at Sutton Harbour are ready to receive them.

UP TRAINS—WEEK DAYS.

Dist. M. C.	STATIONS.	1 Goods. arr.	dep.	2 Goods. arr.	dep.
		a.m.	a.m.	p.m.	p.m.
...	Sutton Harbour	...	8 45	...	6 30
1 2	Friary................	8 50	...	6 35	...

FRIARY AND LAIRA SIDINGS.

UP TRAINS—WEEK DAYS.

Dist. M. C.		1 Goods. arr.	dep.	2 Gds. when required A arr.	dep.	3 Goods. arr.	dep.											
		a.m.	a.m.	p.m.	p.m.	p.m.	p.m.											
... ...	FRIARY Goods Yard	...	7 10	...	4 30	...	6 15	...	...	...	...	...	...	...	...	...	...	...
... 30	Friary Junction	7 13		4 33		6 18		...	...	...	...	...	...	...	...	...	...	...
1 10	Mount Gould Junction	7 14		4 34		6 19		...	...	...	...	...	...	...	...	...	...	...
1 18	LAIRA Sidings	7 15	...	4 35	...	6 20	...	...	...	...	...	...	...	...	...	...	...

DOWN TRAINS—WEEK DAYS.

Dist. M. C.		1 Goods. arr.	dep.	2 Gds. when required A arr.	dep.	3 Goods. arr.	dep.
		a.m.	a.m.	p.m.	p.m.	p.m.	p.m.
... ...	LAIRA Sidings	...	7 40	...	4 43	...	6 35
... 8	Mount Gould Junction	7 42		4 45		6 37	
... 68	Friary Junction	7 43		4 46		6 39	
1 18	FRIARY Goods Yard	7 45	...	4 48	...	6 42	...

A These Trains will run when required and as ordered by Friary.

The Loads of Trains between Laira Sidings and Friary not to exceed 30 Loaded Wagons.

The working timetable for Stonehouse Pool and Sutton Harbour branches, summer 1909.

The GWR's double-track branch to Sutton Harbour passed under the Turnchapel branch south of Friary Junction and bifurcated three quarters of a mile beyond: one line headed to North Quay and Sutton Wharf and the other to the gas works, Sutton Harbour goods depot, a cement works and Bayly's Wharf. Adjacent to the junction of the SR and GWR's Sutton Harbour lines was a signal-post with two arms; the upper one controlled GWR trains and the lower one those of the SR. When a GWR engine entered the harbour lines the upper arm was kept in the clear position until the engine returned. When the GWR arm was clear no SR engine was to pass the SR's Sutton Road level-crossing. Similarly, when the SR signal was clear, no GWR engine was to pass the GWR's Sutton Road level-crossing.

The only surviving broad gauge locomotive, the SDR's vertical boiler 0–4–0WT *Tiny*, now preserved at Buckfastleigh, was built by Sara & Co., Plymouth, in 1868 for the Sutton branch. Unusually its wheelbase of 5 ft 9 in was 1 ft 3¼ in less than the gauge. The tubeless boiler, with a height of 6 ft 3 in and diameter of 2 ft 8½ in, had a vertical flue. Numbered 2180 by the GWR, it was withdrawn in June 1883 and used as a stationary engine in Newton Abbot locomotive shops until 1927, when it was overhauled and placed on the Down platform of the new station.

In standard gauge days 1361 class 0–6–0STs with a short wheelbase of 11 ft were used on the sharply curved dock lines. The LSWR and SR used B4 class 0–4–0Ts on their Sutton Harbour branch, on which gradients limited loads to eight wagons and a brake van.

The Stonehouse Pool Improvement Company's Act of 13 July 1876 permitted the construction of a quay near Poor Man's Point and an associated railway, which was to be worked by the LSWR, running from the authorized Devon & Cornwall Railway's Stonehouse Pool branch. The depth of water allowed ships of 2,000 tons burthen to discharge directly into wagons standing on the quay. A shortage of capital delayed works and the line could not be inspected by the Board of Trade until December 1885, when a certificate was granted. The branch opened to goods on 1 March 1886, but it was to be another eighteen years before passenger trains worked over it.

The LSWR cast envious eyes at the prestigious traffic connected with ocean liners, and when in the autumn of 1903 the American Line announced that all its ships travelling eastwards across the Atlantic would call at Plymouth before reaching the LSWR's docks at Southampton, the LSWR felt it essential to provide facilities at Plymouth to equal those of the GWR. It decided to use Stonehouse Pool Quay, just upstream from the GWR's Millbay Docks. The LSWR, on Stonehouse Pool Improvement Company's land, built a covered 350 ft platform with waiting and refreshment rooms, ticket, inquiry and telegraph offices, and customs and luggage hall. The floors were covered with a cork carpet and the refreshment room was lit by gas and electricity. The station bore bold letters on the roof: 'London South Western Railway' – the 'and' was deliberately omitted to please Americans, who appreciated brevity. A steam crane lifted luggage in specially constructed wheeled crates from the tender's deck to the railway platform. The platform was extended in 1907 to enable two boat trains to be dealt with simultaneously.

The first American Line vessel to call, the *St Louis*, arrived on 9 April 1904. Only passengers were carried by the LSWR as the Post Office refused to take the mail contract from the GWR, whose route via Bristol gave connections to the Midlands and the north of England. On 23 April 1904 the LSWR challenged the GWR boat specials with a luxurious five-coach corridor train which ran from Stonehouse Junction to Waterloo in 4 hours 3 minutes. The vehicles had electric light and were 6 in wider than the LSWR's normal stock. From 1 July 1907 the LSWR took over the Stonehouse Pool Improvement Company.

The SS *Victoria*, a 709 ton vessel built in 1896 for the LSWR's Jersey–St Malo service, was adapted in 1904 for duties as a tender, and visited the same ships as the GWR's tenders. Since acting as tender to transatlantic ships did not fully employ her, during the summer she ran excursions to such places as Dartmouth, Falmouth, Fowey, Looe, Salcombe and Torquay. Being a tender proved to be not always profitable: on 18 February 1907 only eleven passengers disembarked from the SS *New York* and only three used the boat train to Waterloo.

When the White Star Line announced that its vessels would call at Plymouth from 1907, the LSWR realized that traffic would be sufficient for a purpose-built ship and so it ordered the SS *Atalanta*, which was completed in time for the arrival of the SS *Adriatic* from New York on 29 May 1907. The SS *Victoria* returned to the Channel Islands.

The agreement of 13 May 1910 between the LSWR and GWR ended the competitive ocean-liner traffic from Plymouth, so the passenger service from Stonehouse Pool ceased from 28 May 1910. The *Atalanta* was sold to the GWR for use on its Irish service from Fishguard. In 1912 the platform roofing was removed from Stonehouse Pool station and the branch saw no more passenger traffic, apart from possibly a few naval specials.

Boat trains were worked on the branch, which was nearly a mile in length, with an 0–4–4T at the head and an 0–4–0T at the rear. On goods trains the B4 class 0–4–0Ts were limited to a load of nine wagons and a brake van. On 31 December 1960 the last quarter of a mile of the branch was transferred to the British Transport Docks Board; the line carried its last revenue-earning traffic in June 1966 and was closed on 30 May 1970.

The single-track Stonehouse Pool branch left the main line north of Devonport, King's Road station, then descended through a cutting and, in a short tunnel, passed below a corner of the goods shed. After a short tunnel at the foot of Devonport Hill, it curved in an S-bend and passed the Ocean Quay platform to reach Stonehouse Pool Quay.

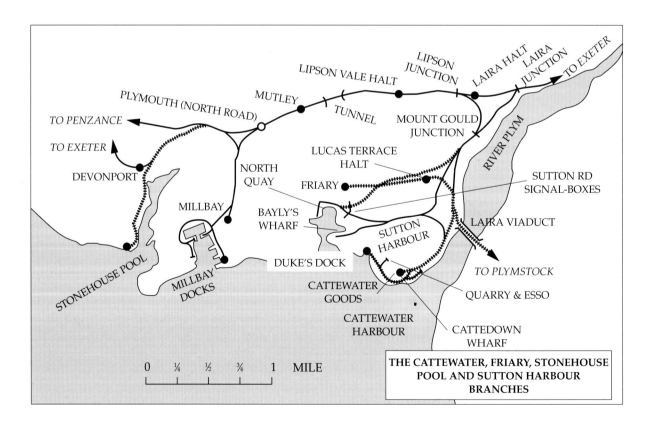

THE CATTEWATER, FRIARY, STONEHOUSE POOL AND SUTTON HARBOUR BRANCHES

B4 class 0–4–0T No. 30102 at Plymouth Friary shed. (No. 30102 is now preserved at Bressingham Gardens.) Notice the spark arrester, which allowed it to work safely in the timber yard at Oreston. Several members of this class shunted in the Plymouth area.

1.7.55 Revd Alan Newman

The LSWR passenger station at Stonehouse Pool built solely for use by ocean liner passengers.

c. 1905 Author's collection

Victoria was used at Plymouth as the LSWR's tender for ocean liner traffic.

c. 1903 Author's collection

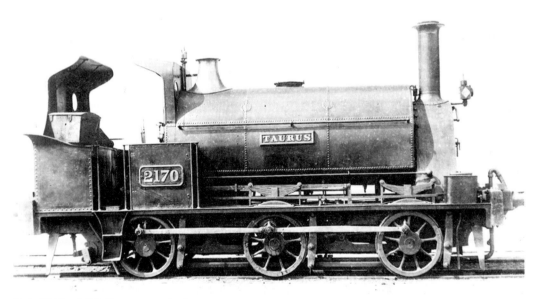

0–6–0T No. 2170 *Taurus* was built in 1869 as a broad gauge engine. In 1892 it was converted to standard gauge and renumbered 1326. Used on the Sutton Harbour line, among other branches, it was scrapped in April 1905.

c. 1890 Author's collection

The Devonport Dockyard Railway

The Royal Naval Dockyards at Devonport extend for 3 miles along the waterfront and cover an area of almost 300 acres; the adjoining barracks accommodate over 2,000 men.

The road to Torpoint Ferry separated the more modern North Yard from the seventeenth-century South Yard, and so to ease communications, in 1857 three tunnels in a distance of about half a mile were opened to link these two yards. From 1876 the 18 ft-wide tunnels carried a single standard gauge railway and a footway. At first horses were used, but in 1869 an Aveling & Porter geared 0–4–0T was used for hauling a wagon through the tunnel.

No. 1, a Hawthorn, Leslie 0–4–0ST built in 1898, was the first normal locomotive to work the dockyard line. In March 1902, when Edward VII and Queen Alexandra visited for the launching of the battleship HMS *Queen*, their saloon was drawn through the tunnel by No. 1, which carried the royal coat of arms in brass. All subsequent dockyard steam locomotives were also 0–4–0STs, except for an 0–4–0T, an ex-crane tank. Four-wheeled diesel-mechanical engines built by F.C. Hibberd & Co. Ltd were introduced in

Four trains at Devonport Dockyard, two steam-hauled and two pulled by F.C. Hibberd diesels.
c. 1955 Hugh Davies

0–4–0ST No. 1, built in 1898 by Hawthorn, Leslie & Co. Ltd, bears the royal coat of arms given when it carried Edward VII and Queen Alexandra in March 1902. No. 1 was scrapped in 1948.

c. 1940 Author's collection

1955 when most of the steam locomotives were retired, though four lasted until the end of passenger services in 1966. Engines were stabled at North Yard in a three-road shed, with corrugated iron in front and stone at the rear. A few locomotives were kept in the South Yard.

When passenger services started in 1900, the 12 ft-high tunnel made special passenger coaches essential. All four-wheelers, they were constructed in the dockyard workshops. Immediately before the withdrawal of passenger services no fewer than six passenger classes were accommodated, and the seating varied from blue upholstery to plain wood. The classes were: Principal Dockyard Officers; Superior and Commissioned Officers; Subordinate Officers; Chief Petty Officers and Chargemen; Recorders and Petty Officers; and Workmen and Ratings. Only the first three classes enjoyed padded seats and lamps. There were six recognized stopping places but no platforms at Extension, Cantilever, North Yard, Central Office, Morice Yard and South Yard.

In 1951 twenty-two Down and twenty-one Up passenger trains were run from Monday to Friday and to midday Saturday, giving a half-hourly service during working hours. Twenty-three minutes were allowed for the 2 mile journey. The passenger service ceased on 16 May 1966, after road improvements rendered the tunnel redundant for passenger purposes. The tunnel and South Yard lines have been out of use since 1982.

Two signal-boxes, one at each end of the tunnel, controlled colour lights. Single-line instruments were installed on the instructions of the Board of Trade after a fatal accident in the tunnel in 1907, when a telegraph boy riding on a truck was killed in a head-on collision between two goods trains. A signalman was required to count the number of vehicles entering the tunnel and inform his colleague at the other end by telegraph, in order to ascertain that no wagons had become uncoupled in transit.

Today two locomotives are in use and there is regular freight transfer from the main line, but no internal traffic. The Dockyard Company has undertaken work for InterCity; in 1994 it fitted secondary door locks to HST Mk 3 coaches, an eight-coach set arriving every week.

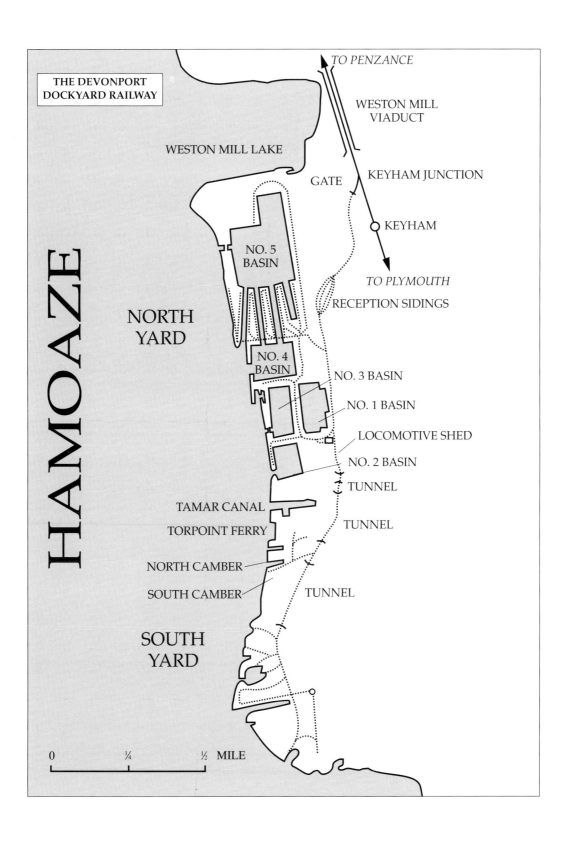

THE DEVONPORT
DOCKYARD RAILWAY

TO PENZANCE

WESTON MILL
VIADUCT

WESTON MILL LAKE

GATE

KEYHAM JUNCTION

KEYHAM

NO. 5
BASIN

TO PLYMOUTH

RECEPTION SIDINGS

NORTH
YARD

HAMOAZE

NO. 4
BASIN

NO. 3 BASIN

NO. 1 BASIN

LOCOMOTIVE SHED

NO. 2 BASIN

TUNNEL

TAMAR CANAL

TORPOINT FERRY

TUNNEL

NORTH CAMBER

SOUTH CAMBER

TUNNEL

SOUTH
YARD

0   ¼   ½   MILE

0–4–0T No. 6 was built by Hawthorn, Leslie & Co. Ltd in 1904 as a crane tank engine. Note the very large solid buffers.

c. 1940 Author's collection

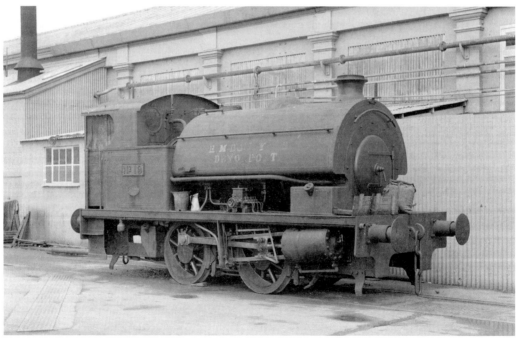

The newest of the dockyard's steam locomotives, No. 19, built by W.G. Bagnall Ltd in 1950. The lettering on the tank reads: 'H.M. Dockyard Devonport'.

c. 1955 Hugh Davies

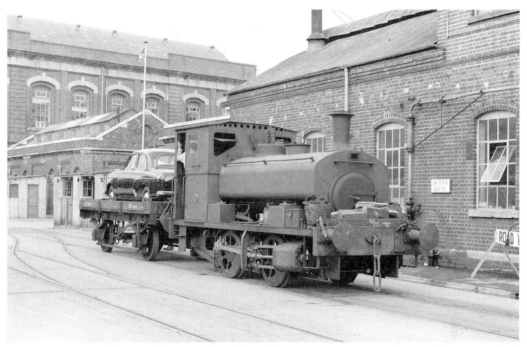

0–4–0ST No. 2, built by Hawthorn, Leslie & Co. Ltd in 1898, at Burma Road. Note the spare sack of coal on the buffer beam.

c. 1955 Hugh Davies

At the exchange sidings at Devonport Dockyard. No. 4858 four-wheel diesel-mechanical, built by F.C. Hibberd & Co. Ltd in 1955, and BR 57XX class 0–6–0PT No. 9711.

c. 1955 Hugh Davies

St Budeaux to Calstock

This branch began as a purely Cornish line, the 3 ft 6 in gauge East Cornwall Mineral Railway, which opened to the public on 7 May 1872. It ran from Calstock Quay, about quarter of a mile east of the present viaduct, up an inclined plane with a gradient of 1 in 6, to a marshalling yard at the top. The line prospered and receipts for the half year ending 30 June 1876 were £2,547 against working expenses of £1,407. On 25 August 1883 the Plymouth, Devonport & South Western Junction Railway secured an Act for building a line from Plymouth to Lydford (thus avoiding the use of the GWR's line between Tavistock Junction and Lydford), and forming a junction with the ECMR at Calstock.

The PDSWJR, leased and worked by the LSWR, opened from Devonport to Bere Alston and Lydford on 2 June 1890. The ECMR was taken over from 1 June 1891; by this time some of the mines had closed and the ECMR was a poorer proposition. As powers for building the Calstock line had lapsed, a Light Railway Order of 12 October 1905 authorized the construction of a link from Bere Alston to Calstock. On 2 March 1908 the ECMR was opened as a standard gauge line. Remarkably, this work was undertaken without suspending traffic for more than two days, and the navvies only had to work on two Sundays. On the same date the new line from Bere Alston to Calstock opened, together with a wagon lift from Calstock Quay to the viaduct; the lift replaced the incline. The LSWR took over the PDSWJR in 1922.

To create an alternative route in case of bomb damage, on 2 March 1941 a link was opened between the GWR's St Budeaux East signal-box and the SR's signal-box at Victoria Road station. The East signal-box was renamed Ferry Road on 27 June 1952 and closed on 2 July 1973. Today the train staff is kept locked in an instrument at St Budeaux, Victoria Road station, and released electrically by a signalman in Plymouth power-box.

St Budeaux to Bere Alston ceased to be a main line on 6 May 1968, when Bere Alston to Meldon Quarry closed. Although closure of the Calstock branch has been considered, it has been kept open, as closure would cause hardship – the roads are narrow, steep, twisting and less direct than the railway. On 7 September 1970 St Budeaux to Bere Alston was singled. The line is now marketed as the Tamar Valley line and offers a most scenic trip.

Beyond St Budeaux the branch passes under the main line to Cornwall and under it once more below the Royal Albert Bridge. On the east side of the line, the Royal Naval Armament Depot Ernesettle sidings came into use on 3 July 1938, and shunting was carried out by the depot's own four-wheel diesel-mechanical locomotives. At the time of writing, a road-rail Mercedes Unimog unit is on site, but the rail connection is unlikely to be used in the future.

Vandalism is not a new phenomenon. It was about here on 30 July 1917 that the

An Up train of three coaches and a guard's van at each end at St Budeaux, Victoria Road.

c. 1908 Author's collection

4.55 p.m. Friary to Tavistock was derailed and turned over as a result of stones having been placed on the line. Five passengers were injured.

The line crosses the seven-span Tamerton Viaduct and passes the site of Tamerton Foliot station, which closed to passengers on 10 September 1962 as roads served the village better. The Tavy Viaduct consists of eight bow-string girders, each spanning 111 ft 4 in, and nine masonry spans of 50 ft. The line climbs at 1 in 73 to Bere Ferrers, where now only the former Down platform is used. The station was the scene of a sad accident on 24 September 1917. A contingent of New Zealand troops travelling by train from Plymouth to Bulford Camp was told that a meal would be provided at the first stop. When the train halted for signals at Bere Ferrers this information was taken literally. The famished soldiers jumped out on the side opposite the platform and ten were killed by the 2.12 p.m. Exeter to Plymouth.

Beyond Bere Ferrers the gradient continues to climb at 1 in 73 to Bere Alston. This formerly had Up and Down main platforms, the far side of the Up platform being used for branch trains to Calstock and Callington. On 7 September 1970 all track, except the Down line, was taken out of use and a new junction put in from the Down line to the branch. Today the driver changes ends while the guard works the points. The single point and the facing point lock are controlled by a two-lever ground frame and released by the One-Train-Working staff. The direction from Plymouth to Bere Alston used to be Up, but with the closure of the through line to Exeter on 6 May 1968 it became Down. Bere Alston was once a favourite place for picnics for Plymouth inhabitants and strawberries were also despatched from the station – 250 tons each season before the Second World War.

Beyond the platform the line falls at 1 in 40 and passengers have a splendid view of the River Tamar, especially as speed is restricted to 15 mph. Calstock Viaduct, an impressive and picturesque structure, consists of massive concrete blocks. There are said to be 11,148 in total, each weighing at least a ton. They were cast on the site and finished to resemble stone. Built by Langs of Liskeard, the twelve arches each have a 60 ft span, the maximum rail height being 120 ft above the river. The viaduct is now a Grade II listed structure.

At the Cornish end of the viaduct was a wagon hoist; with a vertical lift of 113 ft, it was one of the highest in the country. Worked by a steam winding engine, a cage contained the wagon requiring to be lifted or lowered. The cage was nearly balanced by weights, but the cage was slightly heavier. Traffic down to the quay was principally bricks, but also some copper ore and granite, while upwards traffic was coal, timber and limestone. However, the volume of traffic declined and the expense of maintenance could not be justified. The hoist was advertised for sale on 8 September 1934 but was dismantled the following month.

PDSWJR trains normally consisted of three or four coaches. When traffic became heavier, vehicles were borrowed from the LSWR. The company owned sixteen passenger coaches (ex-LSWR and North London Railway), while goods rolling stock consisted of fifty opens, one covered wagon and two brake vans. Usually trains were mixed. In 1913 traffic included 400 tons of arsenic, 5,144 tons of minerals other than coal, and 2,503 head of livestock. Latterly trains consisted of two-coach lattice-gated stock, the large windows of the saloons offering a good view of the scenery. Raids on Plymouth during the Second World War caused some people to move to the countryside and workmen's trains operated with a minimum of four coaches.

The PDSWJR had its own locomotive stud:

BR no.	Wheel arrangement	Name	Notes
30756	0–6–0T	*A.S. Harris*	Named after the company secretary
30757	0–6–2T	*Earl of Mount Edgcumbe*	Named after a director
30758	0–6–2T	*Lord St Leven*	Named after a director

The original blue livery was changed to LSWR green around 1912. The 0–6–2Ts were capable of hauling five bogie coaches, or six in favourable weather, whereas O2 class 0–4–4Ts could only manage four coaches. In PDSWJR days *A.S. Harris* tended to work passenger trains and the 0–6–2Ts the goods services. The loco was moved away from the area during the Second World War, but the other two lasted until the mid-1950s. The O2 class engines were replaced with Ivatt 2–6–2Ts in 1961. The branch was switched to diesel traction on 7 September 1964, but owing to the severe gradients the three-car units usually had the central trailer removed.

In 1910 six trains were run to Calstock and seven in the opposite direction, on weekdays only. Sunday services did not begin until 20 July 1924. By 1938 there were five trains to Calstock and six in the opposite direction, with five each way on Sundays. It was unusual for a branch to have a Sunday service as good as the one on weekdays. In 1951 the six steam-hauled trains on weekdays took 41 to 47 minutes between Plymouth, North Road and Calstock, whereas in 1995, with a reduction of calls and DMU traction, the seven trains do the trip in 32 minutes.

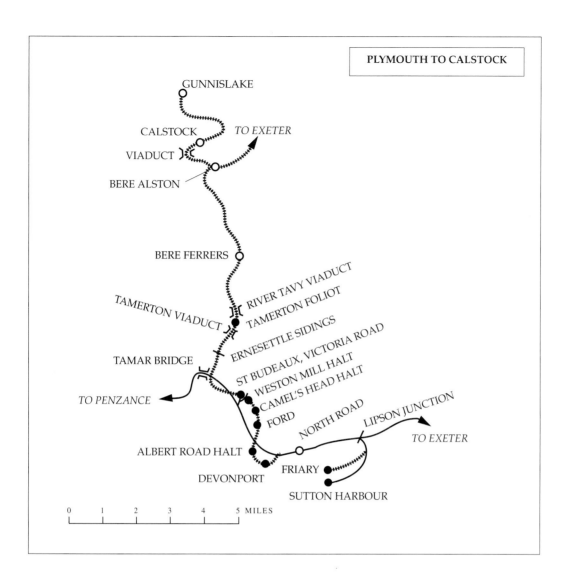

GUNNISLAKE

CALSTOCK

VIADUCT

BERE ALSTON

TO EXETER

BERE FERRERS

TAMERTON VIADUCT

RIVER TAVY VIADUCT

TAMERTON FOLIOT

ERNESETTLE SIDINGS

TAMAR BRIDGE

ST BUDEAUX, VICTORIA ROAD

WESTON MILL HALT

CAMEL'S HEAD HALT

FORD

TO PENZANCE

NORTH ROAD

LIPSON JUNCTION

TO EXETER

ALBERT ROAD HALT

DEVONPORT

FRIARY

SUTTON HARBOUR

PLYMOUTH TO CALSTOCK

0   1   2   3   4   5 MILES

Tamerton Foliot, looking Up. The pair of steps behind the woman has the station name painted on it. Fine pampas grass grows on both platforms.

c. 1911 Author's collection

'West Country' class 4–6–2 No. 34104 *Bere Alston* crosses the River Tavy with the 9.00 a.m. Waterloo–Plymouth Friary.

4.8.60 Hugh Ballantyne

Ex-Plymouth, Devonport & South Western Junction Railway 0–6–2T, now SR No. E758 *Lord St Levan*, at Bere Alston with the 11.28 a.m. to Callington. Note that the coach is gated stock.

31.3.23 Author's collection

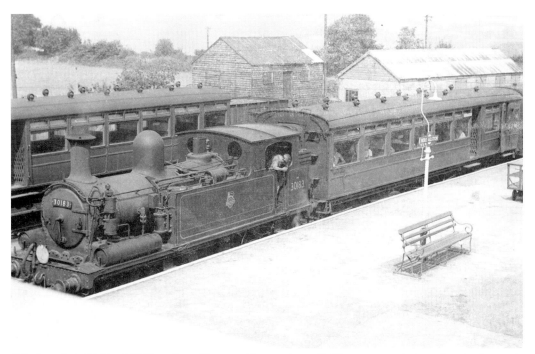

O2 class 0–4–4T No. 30183 at Bere Alston with a train to Callington, consisting of a single coach and utility van. No. 30183 is fitted for motor train working.

1956 M.E.J. Deane

O2 class 0–4–4T No. 30225 stands at Bere Alston with a Callington train, while WR 43XX 2–6–0 No. 6385 passes through with a train from Plymouth to Exeter. It carries the route headcode for Plymouth to Waterloo.

16.8.56 Hugh Davies

The timetable board and Tamar Valley Line logo at Bere Alston.

18.7.94 Author

'Sprinter' 150261 arrives at Bere Alston with the 11.35 a.m. Plymouth–Gunnislake train. It will depart on the line to the right after the guard has worked the ground frame in the foreground (centre left).

18.7.94 Author

The guard works the ground frame at Bere Alston.
18.7.94 Author

BERE ALSTON AND CALLINGTON BRANCH.

This is a Single Line and is worked between Bere Alston and Calstock under the Regulations for working Single Lines by the Train Staff and Ticket, and between Calstock and Callington under the Regulations for working Single Lines by the Electric Train Table Block system.

Distance.		DOWN TRAINS. WEEK-DAYS.	Pass.		Goods. Q		Pass.		Goods.		Pass.		Pass. NS.		Pass. SO.		Pass. NS		Pass. SO		Pass. SO.	
			arr. a.m.	dep. a.m.	arr. a.m.	dep. a.m.	arr. a.m.	dep. a.m.	arr. p.m.	dep. p.m.	arr. p.m.	dep. p.m.	arr. p.m.	dep. p.m.	arr. p.m.	dep. p.m.	arr. p.m.	dep. p.m.	arr. p.m.	dep. p.m.	arr. p.m.	dep. p.m.
M.	c.																					
..	..	**Bere Alston**	..	8 35	..	9 55	..	11 0	..	12 40	..	2 43	..	5 52	..	6 0	..	7 40	..	7 55	..	10 6
1	66	Calstock	8 41	8 44	10×7	10 30	11 6	11 9	12 50	1 0	2 49	2 6½	5 58	6 1	6 6	6 9	7 46	7 49	8 1	8 4	10 11	10 6
4	58	Gunnislake	8 56	8×59	10 45	...	11 21	11X22	1 16	1×50	3 4	3 6	6 13	6 14	6 21	6 24	8 1	8 2	8 16	8 17	10 26	10 27
4	73	Cocking's Siding	...	...	...	...	...	...	A		...	...	...	...	...	...	...	...	...	...	...	...
5	31	Green Hill Siding	...	...	...	...	...	...	A		...	...	...	...	...	...	...	...	...	...	...	...
5	40	Clitters Siding	...	...	...	...	...	...	A		...	...	...	...	...	...	...	...	...	...	...	...
5	12	Chilsworthy	9 3	9 4	...	...	11 26	11 27	A		3 9	3 10	6 18	6 19	6 28	6 29	8 6	8 7	8 21	8 22	10 31	10 32
6	35	Hingston Down Siding	...	...	...	...	...	...	A		...	...	...	...	...	...	...	...	...	...	...	...
6	50	Latchley	9 9	9 9	...	...	11 31	11 32	A		3 14	3 15	6 23	6 24	6 33	6 35	8 11	8 12	8 26	8 27	10 36	10 37
7	63	Luckett	9 13	9 14	...	...	11 36	11 37	A		3 19	3 20	6 28	6 29	6 39	6 42	8 16	8 17	8 31	8 32	10 41	10 42
8	50	Kit Hill Siding	...	...	...	...	...	...	A		...	...	...	...	...	...	...	...	...	...	...	...
9	59	**Callington**	9 19	..	...	...	11 42	...	2 28		3 25	..	6 34	..	6 47	..	8 22	..	8 37	..	10 47	..

Distance.		UP TRAINS. WEEK-DAYS.	Pass.		Goods. A		Pass.		Goods. Q		Pass.		Pass.		Pass. NS		Pass. SO		Pass. SO	
			arr. a.m.	dep. a.m.	arr. a.m.	dep. a.m.	arr. a.m.	dep. a.m.	arr. a.m.	dep. a.m.	arr. p.m.	dep. p.m.	arr. p.m.	dep. p.m.	arr. p.m.	dep. p.m.	arr. p.m.	dep. p.m.	arr. p.m.	dep. p.m.
M.	c.																				
..	..	**Callington**	..	7 10	..	8 0	..	9 55	..	...	..	1 0	..	4 5	..	6 42	..	7 10	..	9 0	...
1	70	Luckett	7 15	7 17	A	...	10 0	10 2	...	...	1 5	1 8	4 10	4 11	6 47	6 48	7 15	7 16	9 5	9 6	...
3	9	Latchley	7 20	7 22	A	...	10 5	10 6	...	...	1 11	1 12	4 14	4 15	6 51	6 52	7 19	7 20	9 9	9 10	...
3	24	Hingston Down Siding	...	...	A	...	...	...	...	...	...	...	...	...	...	...	...	...	...	...	...
4	17	Chilsworthy	7 25	7 27	A	...	10 10	10 11	...	...	1 16	1 17	4 19	4 20	6 56	6 57	7 24	7 25	9 14	9 15	...
5	1	Gunnislake	7 30	7 33	8 40	9×5	10 14	10 16	...	11 30	1X20	1 23	4 23	4 24	7 0	7 1	7 28	7 29	9 18	9 19	...
5	14	Perry, Spear & Co.'s Sidg	...	...	A	...	9 30	10 26	10X28	11 33	11 37	...	...	...	...	...	...	...	...	...	...	...
7	73	Calstock	7 53	7 46	9 20	9 30	10 26	10X28	11 33	12 6	1 33	1 35	4 31	4 36	7 11	7 13	7 39	7 41	9 29	9 31	...
9	59	**Bere Alston**	7 53	..	9 39	...	10 35	...	12 9		1 42	..	4 43	..	7 20	..	7 48	..	9 38	..	...

	DOWN TRAINS. SUNDAYS.	Pass.		Pass.					UP TRAINS. SUNDAYS.	Pass.		Pass.	
		arr. p.m.	dep. p.m.	arr. p.m.	dep. p.m.					arr. a.m.	dep. a.m.	arr. p.m.	dep. p.m.
	Bere Alston	..	12 20	..	8 12	..	..		**Callington**	..	..	..	6 45
	Calstock	12 26	12 29	8 18	8 21	..	..		Luckett	11 5	11 6	6 50	6 51
	Gunnislake	12 41	12 42	8 33	8 34	..	..		Latchley	11 9	11 10	6 54	6 55
	Chilsworthy	12 46	12 47	8 38	8 39	..	..		Chilsworthy	11 14	11 15	6 59	7 0
	Latchley	12 51	12 52	8 43	8 44	..	..		Gunnislake	11 18	11 20	7 3	7 5
	Luckett	12 56	12 57	8 49	8 49	..	..		Calstock	11 35	11 35	7 15	7 18
	Callington	1 9	..	8 54	..	..	..		**Bere Alston**	11 40	..	7 25	..

A—Call when required.

The working timetable, September 1925.

Constructing the piers of Calstock Viaduct.

1907 Lens of Sutton

Calstock Viaduct under construction. Some of the arches are being turned. Note the overhead pulley and transporter.

1907 Author's collection

A wagon lift at Calstock with PDSWJR wagons.

c. 1910 Author's collection

The first Up train to cross Calstock Viaduct. On the far side can be seen the superstructure of the wagon lift.

2.3.08 Author's collection

O2 class 0–4–4T No. 30225 crossing Calstock Viaduct with the 5.23 p.m. Bere Alston–Callington.
4.8.60 Hugh Ballantyne

A two-car DMU works a Gunnislake–Plymouth train across Calstock Viaduct. This view is looking across into Cornwall.

17.8.79 Hugh Ballantyne

Meldon Junction to Halwill Junction and Whitstone & Bridgerule

An Act of 7 July 1873 authorized the construction of the Devon & Cornwall Railway, a single line from Meldon Junction to Holsworthy. The contractor was R.T. Relf of Okehampton, and the line's engineers were W.R. Galbraith and R.T. Church. The branch opened from Meldon to Holsworthy on 20 January 1879, and the LSWR subsidized a horse bus to Bude at £2 per week. This greatly improved Bude's transport links, as prior to the opening of the railway a coach only ran thrice weekly between Okehampton and Bude. The LSWR purchased the Devon & Cornwall Railway on 30 June 1879 and eventually extended it to Whitstone & Bridgerule and Bude on 11 August 1898. Competition from the roads led to the closure of the line to passengers on 3 October 1966.

Before the opening of the branch, Okehampton station was adapted at a cost of about £750 to take Holsworthy trains. At Meldon Junction they branched from the Plymouth line. In the early years of this century, overburden from the top of Meldon Quarry was taken to land at Meldon Junction, where thousands of tons of surplus soil were deposited. The first station on the undulating branch was Maddaford Moor Halt, opened on 26 July 1926 on the site of a passing loop; the loop was open from 1899 until 1921. Situated on the 800 ft contour, the halt had a rare type of waiting shelter, not least in that it was smaller than most.

Ashbury, a two-road station, had stone buildings rendered with cement. It was situated 850 ft above sea level, and oil lamps were still used until its closure. Halwill Junction was a two-road station with a Down bay; an independent North Devon & Cornwall Junction Light Railway platform was added in 1925. A 50 ft locomotive turntable was provided but was little used in its final years. The goods sidings were busy as Halwill was fed by four lines, and various trains converging on it brought wagons to be sorted according to destination. The LSWR slaughterhouse despatched meat, offal, bones and skins by rail. War Department sidings were added at the south end of the station on 26 March 1943 and removed in 1963. At the north end of the station a single line curved round to Ashwater and Padstow. Dunsland Cross had 'Alight here for Shebbear College' added to the station sign; Shebbear College is a Methodist school. The Up loop of the two-road station was taken out of use when the signal-box closed on 2 January 1966.

The line then crossed Holsworthy Viaduct. With nine 50 ft spans, it was the first large viaduct in Britain to be built of concrete, pre-dating 'Concrete Bob' McAlpine's Glenfinnan Viaduct on the West Highland Extension in Scotland. At the west end of the viaduct the track was doubled past an engine shed, where the turntable was taken out of use on 1 January 1911. The adjacent single-road timber engine shed lasted a little longer, but was out of use by 1917. Holsworthy also had an LSWR slaughterhouse and the station generated important livestock traffic. The track then became single again and descended at 1 in 132 to Derriton Viaduct, 176 yd long.

Whitstone & Bridgerule was a two-road station and it was here that for many years tickets were collected from all Down passengers because Bude was an 'open' station. Two War Department sidings were in use from 8 August 1943 to 2 March 1947. Lifting these sidings enabled the Down platform to be lengthened at the Up end. Half a mile beyond the station was Glubb's siding; this served a brick and tile works, which was in use from 1900 to about 1955. Just beyond this point the line entered Cornwall.

Beattie 2–4–0WTs worked the branch in its early days, as did the Adams 46 class 4–4–0Ts. In 1917 Adams 415 class 4–4–2Ts appeared, and O2 and M7 class 0–4–4Ts also worked the branch; Moguls arrived in 1925. T9 class 4–4–0s worked some passenger trains, but Bulleid Pacifics were not permitted until April 1962. The latter were mainly used on Saturday through trains and excursions. Towards the end of steam working, Ivatt and BR Standard tanks were introduced. Diesel power was introduced in September 1964.

The opening timetable for Meldon to Holsworthy offered two passenger and two mixed trains each way on weekdays. In 1887 there were seven Down and six Up trains on weekdays between Meldon and Halwill, taking 26 minutes, and by 1910 one Up train running on Sunday. In 1887, the services took 19 minutes between Halwill and Holsworthy. Two trains each way had connections to or from Bude. In 1910 seven ran each way and one on Sundays, taking 17 minutes to Holsworthy and 10 minutes more to Whitstone. In 1938 there were eight services each way on weekdays and three on

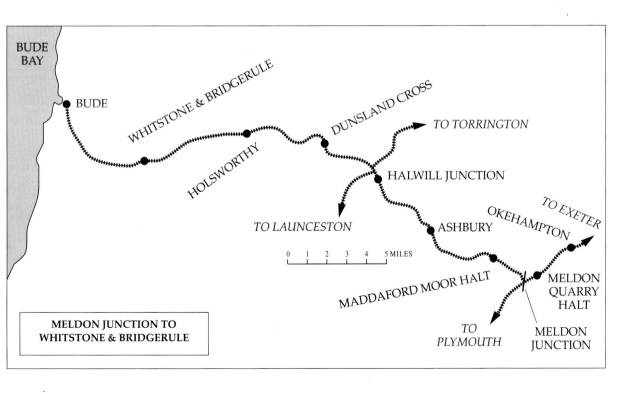

MELDON JUNCTION TO
WHITSTONE & BRIDGERULE

Sundays, with a journey time to Whitstone of 25 minutes. The 1961 timetable showed little variation, with eight Down and seven Up trains on weekdays and four on Sundays.

The Rattlebrook Peat Railway

Four miles south of Meldon Quarry was Bridestowe station, and from a siding trailing off the Down line north of the passenger platform was the Rattlebrook Peat Railway. Opened by the West of England Compressed Peat Company in 1879, the line closed the following year when the firm failed. This standard gauge line passed through many hands and during the First World War a chemical works which used peat was established on the moor, so the line was brought back into working order. The line climbed from 750 ft above sea level at Bridestowe to over 1,800 ft. The direct distance of 2½ miles compared with 6 miles by rail, including a reversal point. Originally worked by a steam locomotive, about which no details are known, a petrol-driven trolley later carried building materials and machinery to the chemical works and also hauled a wagon. The latter doubled as a passenger vehicle and transported workers on day and night shifts. The trolley was used from 1931 to 1932 to salvage the works and dismantle the railway. Subsequently the line was used by lorries to carry peat to Bridestowe station. The last load of peat left about 1955.

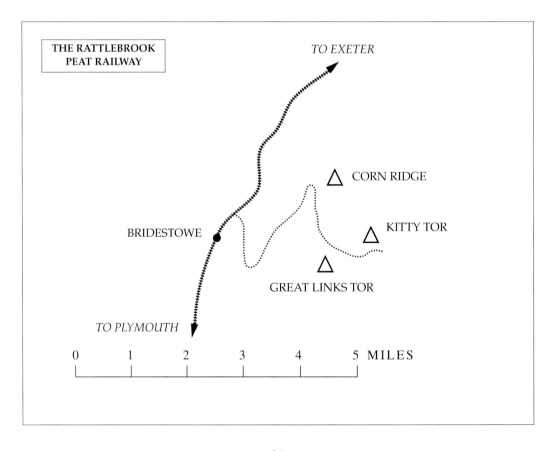

An advertisement for holiday season tickets in the North Devon area, 1934.

A view of Meldon Junction from the cab of the DMU working the 10.05 Okehampton–Bude. The Up line across the viaduct has been taken out of use and a drag installed to protect it.

5.3.66 R.A. Lumber

Messrs S.R. Hawkins and H. Smallacombe outside the combined signal-box and ticket office at Ashbury.

16.3.66 South Western Circle Wessex Collection

An Up Padstow–Exeter goods headed by Adams 0–6–0 No. 442 (involved in the 1885 Yelverton derailment) at Halwill & Beaworthy.

1907 Author's collection

'West Country' class 4–6–2 No. 34020 *Seaton* arriving at Halwill Junction with the 08.30 Padstow–Waterloo.

18.7.64 R.A. Lumber

N class 2–6–0 No. 31841 (72A Exmouth Junction) arriving at Halwill Junction on an Up afternoon train from Padstow to Waterloo. The coaches from Bude are waiting to be backed on, and the porter holds the single-line token. Water churns stand on the platform (left).

23.8.60 R.A. Lumber

BR Standard class 4MT 2–6–4T No. 80037 arrives at Halwill Junction on the 10.12 Okehampton to Padstow and Bude. The rear portion for Bude will be taken forward by No. 80041. No. 80043 had brought in the 09.30 from Bude. The signalman (left) holds a single-line tablet.

18.7.64 R.A. Lumber

'Dunsland Cross. Alight here for Shebbear College.'

16.3.66 South Western Circle Wessex Collection

LSWR Set No. 224, comprising an Up train, leaves Holsworthy. The timber-built engine shed can be seen to the left of the rear coach. Notice the stack of baskets on the Down platform.

c. 1895 Author's collection

Derby three-car suburban DMU, with W50871 leading, stands at Holsworthy.
16.3.66 South Western Circle Wessex Collection

London and South Western Ry.

787

TO

Holsworthy

An LSWR luggage label.

Cattle pens at Holsworthy, built from old rails. A BR petrol pump is to the right.
16.3.66 South Western Circle Wessex Collection

The lorry-loading bay of Holsworthy goods shed. The adjacent goods office is a timber building with a corrugated iron roof.

16.3.66 South Western Circle Wessex Collection

A water crane at Holsworthy.
16.3.66 South Western Circle Wessex Collection

At Whitstone & Bridgerule, T9 class 4–4–0 No. 30715 on a Down train waits to cross an Up train.
23.8.60 R.A. Lumber

Halwill Junction to Launceston

On 28 July 1884 the North Cornwall Railway was authorized by parliament to build a line from Halwill to Padstow via Launceston. Curry & Reeve, the contractors, finished the line so that it could be ceremonially opened on 20 July 1886, for use the following day by the public. The line was extended through to Padstow on 27 March 1899. The North Cornwall Railway was worked and leased by the LSWR and amalgamated with it in 1922. Road transport took its toll of the line's revenue and it closed on 3 October 1966, causing the redundancy of forty-two staff.

Just beyond Halwill Junction, Launceston trains curved south-west. There was a 14 mile descent from 650 ft to 200 ft above sea level on a ruling gradient of 1 in 73 down the valley of the River Carey.

Ashwater had a building of dark stone with round-topped windows, and there was a passing loop and two platforms. To cope with longer trains, the loop was lengthened by 88 yd on 18 October 1936. An economy was made on 7 November 1965, with the closure of the signal-box and passing loop. During 1934 Ashwater signal-box was not opened for the early morning goods and mail train, so before the box closed the previous evening, the signalman was required to release the tablet for Halwill Junction–Ashwater. The tablet was handed to the driver by the early turn signalman at Halwill. Also the previous evening, the Ashwater signalman withdrew the Ashwater–Launceston tablet and deposited it in a slot on top of a special tablet exchange, which was a box fixed in front of the signal-cabin. Before leaving in the evening the signalman set the correct points and signals. When the goods and mail train arrived at Ashwater the driver handed the Halwill–Ashwater tablet to his guard, who placed it in a slot of the special tablet exchange box. This enabled him to withdraw the Ashwater–Launceston tablet, which he then passed to the driver. When the Ashwater signalman arrived in the morning he first checked that the goods and mail train had arrived safely at Launceston, then unlocked the special box and placed the tablet in the normal tablet instrument.

East of Tower Hill was a quarry from where stone for some of the station buildings was extracted. Tower Hill's original layout was almost an exact copy of that at Ashwater. On 15 June 1920 the signal-box and Down platform road were taken out of use, a ground frame working access to the sidings. War Department sidings were added in 1943 and the volume of wartime traffic demanded the restoration of the signal-box and loop. A new signal-box was provided in the office on the Up platform. The Down loop was taken out of use again on 7 November 1965.

One and a half miles east of Launceston the line crossed the River Tamar into Cornwall over Polston Bridge, which was built of girders on granite-faced piers.

During the summer the branch was busy with holidaymakers going to and from such places as Wadebridge and Padstow. Goods traffic included china clay from Bodmin Moor and slate from Delabole. The 24 tons of fish from Padstow in 1900 rose to 3,074 tons in 1911; 750 containers of fresh meat and 625 truck loads of cattle left Launceston in 1957.

The first engines to work the branch were Beattie 2–4–0WTs, followed by Adam's radial tanks and 'Jubilee' class 0–4–2 tender engines. Later still, M7 class 0–4–4Ts and T9 4–4–0s appeared, while N class 2–6–0s worked some trains from 1924 onwards. Weight restrictions over Meldon Viaduct, and the fact that Padstow had a short turntable, meant that the heaviest engines were 2–6–0s, until a 70 ft diameter turntable was put in at Padstow in April 1947. After that date 'West Country' class engines worked some trains. Only non-rebuilt engines could be used, as the rebuilds were too heavy for Little Petherick Viaduct, near Padstow. The T9s lasted until July 1961, while the Pacifics and the N classes ceased working the branch in 1964; only BR Standard class 4 4–6–0s were left prior to the introduction of diesel working.

The timetable remained constant for much of the branch's existence. The service of six Down and five Up trains lasted well into the twentieth century, though the journey time for the 13½ miles between Halwill and Launceston had been reduced from 31 minutes in 1887 to 24 minutes by 1910. The 1961 timetable showed six Down and seven Up trains for weekdays and three each way on Sundays. The time allowed was still about 24 minutes.

At Ashwater, a three-coach Up passenger train overtakes a goods train. The latter comprises at least eight cattle trucks, and the engine is shunting the yard.

c. 1905 Author's collection

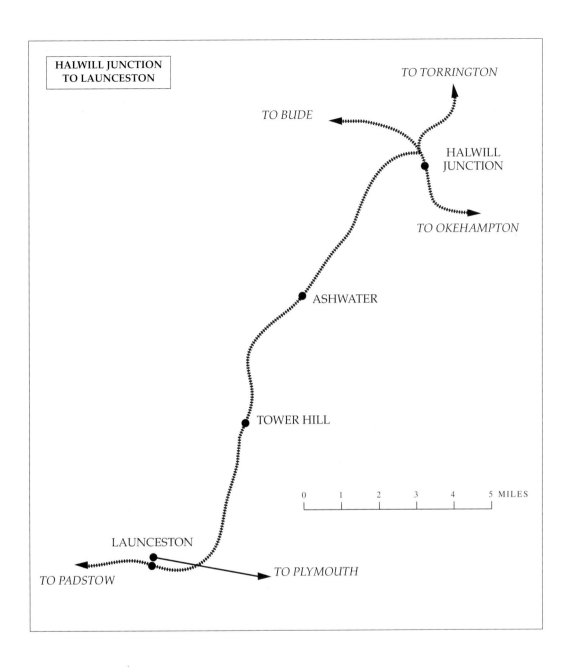

TO TORRINGTON

TO BUDE

HALWILL
JUNCTION

**HALWILL JUNCTION
TO LAUNCESTON**

TO OKEHAMPTON

ASHWATER

TOWER HILL

0   1   2   3   4   5 MILES

LAUNCESTON

TO PADSTOW

TO PLYMOUTH

Ashwater, a view looking in the Up direction. Opposite the goods shed, in the distance, is a store. An LSWR cattle truck stands on the far left, having been lime washed after the unloading of the cattle.

c. 1905 Author's collection

At Ashwater, T9 class 4–4–0 No. 30710, on the 3.13 p.m. Padstow–Exeter, crosses 'West Country' class 4–6–2 No. 34031 *Torrington* on a Down train.

20.8.58 E. Wilmshurst

'Battle of Britain' class 4–6–2 No. 34066 *Spitfire* collects the single-line tablet at Ashwater while working the Up 'Atlantic Coast Express'.

11.7.64 R.A. Lumber

A single-car DMU at Ashwater on an Up working.

16.3.66 South Western Circle Wessex Collection

A three-car DMU, working the 11.55 Halwill Junction–Wadebridge, calls at Tower Hill after it had been reduced to a halt. Only the former Up road is in use, the signal-box having closed on 7 November 1965.

3.9.66 R.A. Lumber

London and South Western Ry.

787

From_____

TO

Launceston

An LSWR luggage label.

Barnstaple to Halwill Junction

The branch between Barnstaple and Halwill was built piecemeal. The first section was constructed by the Taw Vale Railway & Dock Company, which obtained an Act of 21 July 1845 to build docks at Fremington and a line to Barnstaple. Opened on 25 April 1848, it was horse-worked until 1 August 1854, the same day as the North Devon Railway between Barnstaple and Crediton opened. On that day broad gauge steam engines began working from Crediton to Fremington.

The Bideford Extension Railway Act was passed on 4 August 1853. The contractor, and main subscriber, for the broad gauge line was Thomas Brassey. The first sod was cut on 20 August 1853 and the opening celebrations held at Bideford on 29 October 1855. Three hundred guests travelled free – no charge could be made as the Board of Trade had yet to grant a certificate authorizing the line to be used by paying passengers. Most guests stayed for a ball and intended to return home on the 9.00 p.m. train, but this passed through the station, stopped to collect a few privileged passengers and moved on. The hundred merrymakers left on the platform had to walk, hire vehicles, lodge at Bideford, or camp at the station until the next morning. Fares were taken from 2 November 1855.

Brassey leased the North Devon and the Bideford Extension lines, operating them as one. The LSWR took over both railways on 1 August 1862, and the company was amalgamated on 1 January 1865. The LSWR, being a standard gauge company, arranged that mixed gauge should reach Bideford on 2 March 1863, although a daily broad gauge train ran to Bideford until 1877. An Act was passed on 19 June 1865 to extend the line to Torrington. Three years later the LSWR tried to abandon the line as it had calculated that the cost of construction would not warrant the expenditure. The fact that the Hon. Mark Rolle, the canal proprietor, actually opposed the granting of powers for abandonment and pressed for a railway, against the wishes of the railway company itself, is probably unique.

The contractor, James Taylor, began work around April 1870, using part of the formation of the Rolle Canal, which had opened in 1825. The LSWR opened to Torrington on 18 July 1872, without celebrations.

The 3 ft gauge Marland Light Railway was planned to carry china clay to the LSWR at Torrington. Its engineer was John Barraclough Fell, inventor of the Fell centre rail used on various lines, including the one opened in 1868 over the Mount Cenis Pass. The Marland Light Railway opened in 1880 and, in addition to clay, carried coal, agricultural produce and bricks. An average of 100 tons of clay was carried daily in 3½ ton wagons and eight men were employed on transfer work at Torrington. Workmen's services used two ex-London horse trams and two open wagons, covered and fitted with seats.

The MLR had quite a variety of locomotives, including three Fletcher, Jennings & Co. 0–4–0STs purchased from the contractors of the St Helier Breakwater. These had their saddle tanks removed and placed on a wagon behind the engine in order to lighten the load on the fragile 135 ft-long timber Torrington Viaduct. They were painted unlined dark green.

The North Devon & Cornwall Junction Light Railway, which despite its name lay wholly in Devon, obtained a Light Railway Order on 28 August 1914 to build a line between Torrington and Halwill Junction, partly on the formation of the MLR. However, the outbreak of war delayed its construction. On 12 April 1922 the scheme was revived and an extension of time was granted on 27 February 1924. The original contractors, Messrs McAlpine, withdrew and it was taken over by P.W. Anderson. A large proportion of the tender was paid in shares at a discounted price and in February 1925 Anderson went bankrupt. The NDCJLR's directors paid themselves expenses in shares as so little money was available.

To alleviate unemployment following the First World War, the Treasury contributed £125,000, on condition that men supplied by the Labour Exchange were used. Devon County Council and Bideford Corporation also gave financial assistance. The unskilled labour came from Plymouth and Devonport, and Col. H.F. Stephens, the line's engineer, provided hutments for accommodation.

When the first sod was ceremonially cut on 30 June 1922 construction was expected to take twenty months, but the very wet summers of 1923 and 1924 caused the work to take almost three years. The Board of Trade inspected the line on 10 and 11 July 1925 and the NDCJLR opened to the public on 27 July. Apart from the Westbury and Frome avoiding lines, it was the last major railway construction in the west of England. The NDCJLR was worked by the SR, but remained nominally independent until nationalization in 1948.

The opening of the NDCJLR led to the truncation of the Marland Light Railway near Dunsbear Halt, but several miles of 3 ft gauge line were retained around Peters Marland to take clay to the works. Later, John Fowler four-wheel diesel-mechanical locomotives were used, until the closure of the 3 ft gauge system on 13 November 1970.

A survey on 7 May 1963 revealed that the average number of passengers on trains between Barnstaple and Torrington was just over nine. On the Torrington to Halwill line even one passenger on one of the two daily trains was a rarity. A second survey revealed the shortfall:

June 1963	Expenses (£)	Earnings (£)
Torrington to Halwill	53,000	1,000
Torrington to Barnstaple	100,000	10,000

Consequently the Halwill–Torrington passenger service was withdrawn. In addition, Halwill–Meeth closed to all traffic on 1 March 1965 and Torrington–Barnstaple closed to passengers on 4 October 1965, though Bideford–Torrington was temporarily re-opened from 10 to 22 January 1968 as an emergency measure when flood damage to Bideford Bridge caused part of it to collapse. During this period the two areas of Bideford divided by the river were linked by an hourly train service from Bideford to Torrington and by bus from Torrington station to the west end of Bideford – a circuitous route of about 11 miles.

Milk traffic from Torrington ceased on 7 May 1973 but the clay trains continued. The following year Unigate Dairies started using rail again and three clay trains were run daily. Milk traffic ceased permanently in 1978 and by 1981 clay traffic consisted of only one 57 tonne wagon, filled daily. The branch closed on 31 August 1982, when necessary repairs to an underline bridge would have been uneconomic, and clay was then transported by road to the railhead at Okehampton. In 1980 a local action committee organized charter passenger trains from Bideford. Devon County Council has recently converted the trackbed from Barnstaple to Meeth into a footpath and cycleway.

Barnstaple Junction had two through passenger platforms, and a Down loop was brought into use in 1924. (For more details of the station see page 116.)

West of the station the line became single. A passing loop was provided at Fremington, which was important for its quay where locomotive coal from South Wales was landed and distributed to LSWR sheds in the south-west; 50,000 tons of coal arrived annually. The port was modernized by the SR between the wars, and in Devon the port was second only to Plymouth. Cranes were provided for transferring clay from railway wagon to ship, and in 1933 1,220 tons of clay for Spain were loaded in four days. The quay closed on 30 March 1970 and all the sidings were taken out of use. Beyond the yard was Fremington Pill Viaduct, 82 yd long.

East Yelland CEGB power station siding, opened around 1949, was little used as most of the coal came by sea, and it closed in 1973. Beyond was the 83 yd Instow Tunnel. Instow signal-box, now preserved and Grade II listed, controlled the level crossing. The waterside station was beyond and from here sugar beet and pit props were transported.

The original passenger station at Bideford (closed on 10 June 1872) was nearer the River Torridge and not far from the site of the later goods shed in the extensive goods yard. A replacement station called Bideford New opened when the line was extended to Torrington. It was built south-west of the town and was closer than the old station. In 1928 60,117 tickets were issued and 106,762 collected, whereas eight years later the respective figures were 33,292 and 92,618. Although passenger traffic *from* Bideford fell as a result of competition from buses, arrivals were not so badly affected. The station has recently been restored and most of it is used for administering County Parks projects. Some track has been relaid and a replica signal-box built.

The line past Bartlett's siding was brought into use in 1915 and it also served the explosives firm of Kynock Limited. It then crossed a 135 yd-long viaduct over the River Torridge and further on was the 196 yd Landcross Tunnel.

For many years Torrington was a terminus and the transhipment point with the Marland Light Railway until this was replaced by the NDCJLR. The station had a single-road engine shed built of timber. This was erected in 1872 and accommodated two small tender engines. It closed in November 1959. The station had thirty-five staff in SR days. Torrington had the West Country's largest creamery, which sent 2 million gallons of milk to London in 1957. The original milk depot, installed in 1940, was resited on the Up platform in 1974. An ICI fertilizer store opened on 20 April 1978 on the site of the Down platform and goods shed. Bagged fertilizer arrived by rail and was subsequently distributed over a wide area by road.

Beyond the station the line crossed the River Torridge on a nine-span steel girder bridge, then ascended at 1 in 45. Beyond Watergate Halt (opened on 20 September 1926 and with no shelter) was Yarde Halt, which marked the summit of the line. Opened on 19 July 1926, it had a concrete shelter at the foot of the platform ramp. Further along from Dunsbear Halt was Marland siding where Guard S. Rowlands was killed in a shunting accident. (It was he who had suggested the name 'Atlantic Coast Express' for the 11.00 a.m. from Waterloo.) The last clay by rail left Marland siding in 1968.

Petrockstow station, built of stone, had a passing loop until 26 February 1967, when the Down loop was reduced to a siding. Outward traffic was timber and cattle, while fertilizers, coal and feedstuffs were the incoming products. There were more clay sidings at Meeth and the halt was sited about a mile further on. Hatherleigh had a stone building on the platform and was also provided with a passing loop. The station was situated 2 miles from the town and a journey to Okehampton, the nearest large town, was 20 miles by rail, yet only seven by road! Hole also had a stone building and passing loop. Approaching Halwill Junction the line ran parallel with the Bude branch, and NDCJLR passenger trains used an independent shelterless platform west of the main passenger station.

Most broad gauge North Devon Railway locomotives were ex-Bristol & Gloucester Railway engines purchased by Brassey when the Midland Railway converted the line to mixed gauge. The ex-BGR locomotives were bought for about £1,000 each. There were five 2–2–2s, one 2–4–0 and two 0–6–0s. Another four engines were obtained from other sources. NDR locomotive livery was brown with yellow bands and lining.

Records show that in 1872 'Volcano' class 2–4–0 No. 25 *Reindeer* and 'Falcon' class 2–4–0 No. 84 *Styx*, both from Yeovil shed, ran through to Torrington. From 1874 'Eagle' class 2–4–0s No. 27 *Eagle*, No. 28 *Hawk* and No. 30 *Vulture* appeared on the branch, as did Ilfracombe Goods 0–6–0s. By the mid-1880s Beattie well tanks and Adams Radials worked some services. In the late 1890s Adams 380 class 4–4–0s could be seen. These were nicknamed 'Steamrollers', probably because of the deep rumbling noise they made when coasting down gradients. T3 class 4–4–0s also appeared around this time.

In the SR era E1R class 0–6–2Ts, M7 class 0–4–4Ts and N class 2–6–0s were common. In the BR period Ivatt class 2P 2–6–2Ts were seen from 1953, and later BR Standard class 3 2–6–2Ts and class 4 2–6–4Ts appeared. DMUs arrived in 1964.

At first the NDCJLR was worked by Adams 460 class 4–4–0s but these were at a serious disadvantage because the turntable at Halwill was on the opposite side of the line to the NDCJLR. When Wadebridge and Bude trains simultaneously occupied the other roads, access to the turntable was blocked and so the journey back to Torrington had to be made tender-first – something a crew tried to avoid as it was unpleasant.

In August 1926 ex-PDSWJR 0–6–2T No. 758 *Lord St Levan* was tested on the branch and Hawthorn, Leslie was asked to tender for six engines of this type. However, to reduce expenditure, ex-London, Brighton & South Coast Railway E1 class 0–6–0Ts were rebuilt from 1927 to 1928 using trailing axles which were spare from the War Office contract for building N class 2–6–0s. They also had enlarged bunkers and were re-classified E1R. They hauled a single LSWR ex-steam railcar trailer saloon. Barnstaple shed usually had Nos 2094/5, 2608, 2610/6, three of these being outshedded at Torrington. When the E1Rs were put on the Torrington portion of the 'Atlantic Coast Express' their fore and aft motion gave cause for concern and the balance weights on the driving wheels had to be modified.

The SR provided rolling stock for the NDCJLR. Workmen used coach No. 741, kept at Petrockstow during the day. It was a flat-roofed saloon which had been converted from one of the first steam railcars.

Timetables for the Barnstaple to Torrington line show an increased service frequency and shorter travelling times over the years:

1887   8 Down and 7 Up weekdays, taking about 45 minutes for the 14 miles
1910   10 Down and 10 Up, taking about 44 minutes
1938   14 Down and 10 Up; Sundays 6 Down and 8 Up, taking 30 to 35 minutes
1961   12 Down and 11 Up; Sundays 7 Down and 6 Up

In 1925 the NDCJLR ran five trains each way, many of them mixed. In 1938 two ran each way from Halwill to Torrington, plus one from Hatherleigh to Torrington, taking about 1 hr 25 mins for the 20½ miles. In 1961 two trains daily were provided each way, plus one Torrington–Petrockstow and return. In the DMU period there were interesting through workings: Barnstaple–Halwill, Taunton–Torrington and Torrington–Salisbury.

The branch was one of the very few in the British Isles to be patrolled by an armoured train. Following the evacuation of Dunkirk in July 1940 it was believed that the beaches near the mouth of the River Taw offered potential sites for a German invasion. To help prevent such an action, an armoured train patrolled between Bideford and Braunton on the Ilfracombe line. An LMS locomotive coal wagon formed the basis of the armoured truck, the main armament being a six-pounder, 6 cwt Hotchkiss Mark II gun, introduced in 1917 for tanks. Between this armoured truck and the front of the engine was a supply van. The locomotive, ex-LNER F4 class 2–4–2T No. 7077, had been suitably armoured. Behind the engine's bunker was an ammunition van and an armoured wagon with rifles and Bren light machine guns. The locomotive was maintained by SR staff at Barnstaple Junction. The army footplate crew was required to pass the SR's rules and regulations test to the satisfaction of the District Locomotive Superintendent. By the spring of 1942 fears that the south-west peninsula would be invaded had receded and on 20 April 1942 the armoured train was moved to Tilbury.

The branch was the scene of several mishaps. On 4 January 1859 the North Devon Railway 2–2–2 *Taw* with two coaches was working the 6.15 p.m. Exeter–Bideford when a driving wheel tyre broke, derailing the tender and first coach. It is believed that *Taw* was an ex-North Midland Railway standard gauge engine converted to run on the broad gauge.

On 23 September 1869 a collision occurred at Fremington between the 3.15 p.m. broad gauge mixed train from Bideford to Crediton and the 1.25 p.m. standard gauge passenger train from Exeter to Bideford. The collision was blamed on the pointsman and driver of the Down passenger service. On 19 October 1890 2–4–0WT No. 254 in Bideford goods yard uptipped three wagons loaded with manure, and in 1951 the sparsity of traffic in the area was revealed when an NDCJLR train, carrying a driver, fireman, guard and one passenger, collided on an ungated level crossing with a bus carrying a driver, conductor and no passengers.

A Barnstaple Junction platform ticket.

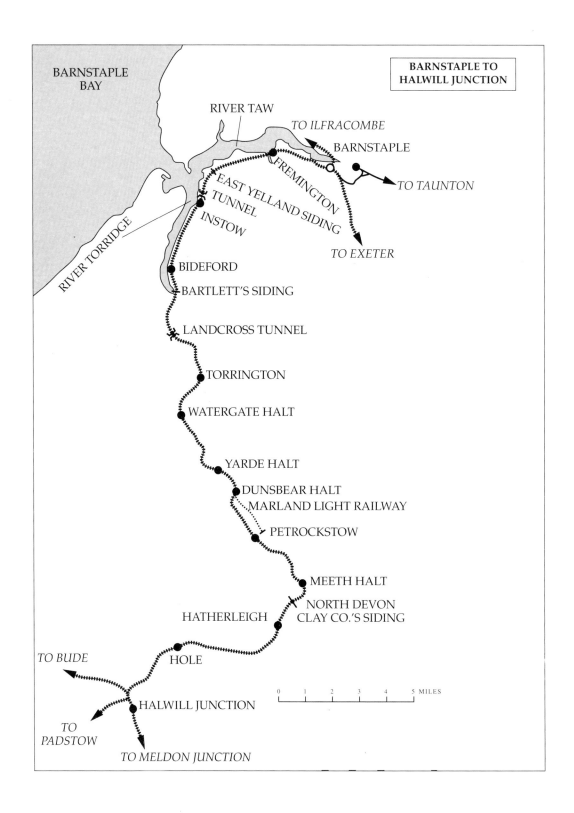

BARNSTAPLE BAY

RIVER TAW

TO ILFRACOMBE

BARNSTAPLE TO
HALWILL JUNCTION

BARNSTAPLE

FREMINGTON

TO TAUNTON

EAST YELLAND SIDING

TUNNEL

TO EXETER

INSTOW

RIVER TORRIDGE

BIDEFORD

BARTLETT'S SIDING

LANDCROSS TUNNEL

TORRINGTON

WATERGATE HALT

YARDE HALT

DUNSBEAR HALT

MARLAND LIGHT RAILWAY

PETROCKSTOW

MEETH HALT

NORTH DEVON
CLAY CO.'S SIDING

HATHERLEIGH

TO BUDE

HOLE

0 1 2 3 4 5 MILES

HALWILL JUNCTION

TO
PADSTOW

TO MELDON JUNCTION

Fremington, looking east. A steamship is moored at the quay, with coal wagons alongside headed by an Adams 4–4–0. Beyond is a four-masted sailing ship.

c. 1930 Lens of Sutton

The 13.15 Barnstaple–Torrington service at Fremington, headed by Ivatt class 2 2–6–2T No. 41290. The boilers of the steam cranes were checked by a boiler inspector from Eastleigh. The signal-box is of an unusual design.

15.8.64 E. Wilmshurst

Class E1R 0–6–2T No. B94 at Instow with a Down train.

c. 1930 A. Halls

Crowds welcome the first train to Bideford. Note the triumphal arch, flags, and disc and crossbar signal. The station in the distance is the original waterside terminus.

29.10.1855 Courtesy *Illustrated London News*

M7 class 0–4–4T No. 30245 (now preserved by the National Railway Museum) arrives at Bideford from Torrington with seven milk tanks in front of the passenger coaches.

5.8.52 R.E. Toop

A general view of Torrington with the passenger station to the left and goods shed in the centre. Two engines stand outside the shed located to the left of the far end of the passenger train. On the right, beyond the kissing gate and between two roads of standard gauge wagons, can be seen the transfer siding and 3 ft gauge wagons of the Marland Light Railway.

c. 1920 Author's collection

Ivatt class 2 2–6–2T No. 41249, having worked a passenger train from Barnstaple Junction, is having its tanks replenished at Torrington. It is crossing an Up train.

15.8.64 E.Wilmshurst

On the 3 ft gauge Marland Light Railway, a Black Hawthorn 0–6–0ST crosses the timber viaduct at Torrington. The first two coaches are ex-London horse trams, while the last two are converted open wagons.

c. 1920 Author's collection

North British type 2 diesel-hydraulic D6349 stands at Torrington before working the 08.52 Torrington–Barnstaple Junction service.

22.2.65 Author's collection

M7 class 0–4–4T No. 30250 working a Down passenger train at Torrington.

c. 1955 Lens of Sutton

A single-car DMU working the 08.55 Torrington–Halwill Junction calls at Petrockstow. The building between the station offices and the train was a cattle-feed store.

22.2.65 Author's collection

Constructing the North Devon & Cornwall Junction Light Railway.

c. 1923 Author's collection

NORTH DEVON & CORNWALL JUNCTION LIGHT RAILWAY.

This is a Single Line and is worked under Tyer's Train Tablet System (No. 6 Instruments).

Distance M	Distance C	WEEKDAYS.	Mixed. Conveys Workmen. arr. a.m.	dep. a.m.	Goods. arr. a.m.	dep. a.m.	Mixed. arr. a.m.	dep. a.m.	Goods. C arr. p.m.	dep. p.m.
...	...	Torrington	...	6 30	...	8 20	...	9 0	...	12 15
1	75	Watergate Siding	...	...	...	...	...	...	C	...
...	...	Yarde	6 51	6 52	...	...	...	...	...	...
5	59	Dunsbear Halt	...	...	...	...	9 24	9 25	...	...
6	02	Clay Company's Siding	6 56	...	...	...	...	...	12 41	12 55
7	78	Petrockstow	...	...	8 54	...	9 34	9 57	1 3	1 15
9	65	N. Devon Clay Company's Siding	...	...	...	...	...	...	1 21	1 35
10	55	Meeth Halt	...	...	...	...	9 46	9 47	C	...
12	65	Hatherleigh	...	...	...	...	9 56	9 58	1 47	2 2
17	49	Hole	...	...	...	...	10 16	10 17	2 30	2 31
20	53	Halwill	...	...	...	...	10 26	...	2 40	...

WEEKDAYS.	Mixed. arr. p.m.	dep. p.m.	Mixed. arr. p.m.	dep. p.m.	Goods. Q arr. p.m.	dep. p.m.	Goods. Q arr. p.m.	dep. p.m.
Torrington	...	3 5	...	5 25	...	6 5	...	6 5
Watergate Siding	...	...	...	...	...	...	...	...
Yarde	...	...	...	...	...	...	...	...
Dunsbear Halt	3 29	3 30	5 49	5 50	...	...	...	...
Clay Company's Siding	...	...	...	...	6 39	6 49	6 39	...
Petrockstow	3 39	3 42	5 59	6 2	6 57	...	...	...
N. Devon Clay Company's Siding	...	...	...	...	...	...	...	...
Meeth Halt	3 51	3 52	6 11	6 12	...	...	...	...
Hatherleigh	4 X1	4 3	6 21	6 23	...	...	...	...
Hole	4 21	4 22	6 41	6 42	...	...	...	...
Halwill	4 31	...	6 51	...	...	...	...	...

Distance M	Distance C	WEEKDAYS.	Goods. arr. a.m.	dep. a.m.	Goods. arr. a.m.	dep. a.m.	Mixed. A arr. a.m.	dep. a.m.	Goods. arr. p.m.	dep. p.m.
...	...	Halwill	...	...	...	...	...	10 46	...	3 10
3	04	Hole	...	...	...	...	10 55	10 56	3 19	3 34
7	68	Hatherleigh	...	...	...	...	11 13	11 15	3 51	4 X 9
9	78	Meeth Halt	...	...	...	...	11 24	11 25	...	...
10	68	N. Devon Clay Company's Siding	...	...	...	...	...	...	4 21	4 30
12	55	Petrockstow	...	...	...	9 40	11 34	11 35	4 36	4 46
14	51	Clay Company's Siding	...	7 22	9 48	10 28	...	...	...	...
14	74	Dunsbear Halt	...	...	...	...	11 44	11 45	...	...
...	...	Yarde	...	...	...	...	A		...	...
18	58	Watergate Siding	...	...	...	...	...	...	...	...
20	53	Torrington	7 57	...	10 57	...	12 10	...	5 21	...

WEEKDAYS.	Mixed. B. arr. p.m.	dep. p.m.	Goods. arr. p.m.	dep. p.m.	Goods. Q.C. arr. p.m.	dep. p.m.	Mixed. arr. p.m.	dep. p.m.
Halwill	...	4 55	...	...	...	...	...	7 35
Hole	5 4	5 5	...	...	...	...	7 44	7 45
Hatherleigh	5 23	5 24	...	...	...	...	8 2	8 4
Meeth Halt	5 33	5 34	...	...	...	...	8 13	8 14
N. Devon Clay Company's Siding	...	...	...	...	...	...	...	...
Petrockstow	5 43	5 44	...	...	...	7 15	8 23	8 24
Clay Company's Siding	...	...	...	6 50	7 23	7 35	...	...
Dunsbear Halt	5 53	5 54	...	...	C	...	8 33	8 34
Yarde	6 0	6 1	...	...	...	...	...	...
Watergate Siding	B	...	...	...	...	...	...	...
Torrington	6 22	...	7 19	...	8 4	...	8 59	...

A.—Calls at Yarde to set down Workmen S.O.   B.—Does not call at Yarde S.O.
C.—Call if required.

The North Devon & Cornwall Junction Light Railway working timetable, September 1925.

111

Ivatt class 2 2–6–2T No. 41298 (now preserved at the Buckinghamshire Railway Centre), with a short Down freight train, crosses an ungated level crossing at Meeth. The cast iron notice reading 'Beware of Trains' is not very prominent.

14.8.56 R.E. Toop

Adams 460 class 4–4–0 No. 475A at Hatherleigh. In July 1925 seven engines of this class were transferred to Barnstaple for the opening of the NDCJLR. No. 475 was withdrawn from service in February 1926.

c. 1925 Author's collection

A single-car DMU working the 08.55 Torrington–Halwill Junction service at Hole.

22.2.65 Author's collection

E1R class 0–6–2T No. 2095 after its arrival at the NDCJLR platform, Halwill Junction.

c. 1930 Lens of Sutton

Exeter to Barnstaple

This was another branch built in sections. Following the passing of the Exeter & Crediton Railway Act on 21 July 1845, Messrs Waring set to work on the building contract. Early in 1847 the double-track broad gauge line was finished except for the construction of a junction with the Bristol & Exeter Railway at Cowley Bridge. However, the line was prevented from being opened by the LSWR, which craftily purchased the majority of shares and outvoted the Exeter & Crediton directors. This must have been particularly annoying for the host of the Ship Hotel, Crediton, who had laid in great stocks of champagne and bought a feeder omnibus ready for the opening.

Meanwhile, the Taw Vale Extension Railway, backed by the LSWR, had laid standard gauge track from Barnstaple to Fremington and relaid the Exeter & Crediton to standard gauge. When this had been done the Railway Commissioners, who had been considering the gauge of the Taw Vale Extension, decided in February 1848 that it should be broad gauge. The Exeter & Crediton was left derelict until early spring 1851, when one track was reconverted to broad gauge and leased to the B&ER; the other road was left as standard gauge. Capt. Wynne carried out the Board of Trade inspection on 8 May 1851 and the Exeter & Crediton was ceremonially opened on 12 May 1851. Crediton was decorated with flowers, trees and triumphal arches.

The Taw Vale Extension Railway Act for building a line from Barnstaple to Crediton was passed on 7 August 1846. As mentioned above, the deliberations on the line's gauge delayed matters. On 24 July 1851 an Act changed the company's name to the North Devon Railway & Dock Company. It was not until 2 February 1852 that the first sod was ceremonially cut at Copplestone and the contractor, William Brassey, set to work. the broad gauge line from Crediton to Fremington Pill was inspected by the Board of Trade on 29 June 1854 and the ceremonial opening took place on 12 July, when about a thousand guests sat down to dinner in the new Market Hall at Barnstaple. When the line was opened to the public on 1 August, rolling stock was provided by the B&ER. Brassey then took over on 28 July 1855. The LSWR appropriated the leases of the NDR and Bideford Extension on 31 July 1862 and the NDR amalgamated with the LSWR on 1 January 1865. The Exeter & Crediton was taken over by the LSWR on 26 June 1879.

An accident occurred at Copplestone on 16 July 1861, when thirteen passengers and a guard were injured. Although the station had a crossing loop, there was only one platform. When trains were to cross, the procedure was for the first to be turned into the platform road on the loop, while the second train remained on the platformless main line before shunting to the platform when the first train left. On this occasion the signalman carelessly turned the second train into the platform loop, where it struck the first. The signalman was imprisoned for a month.

The broad gauge service from Crediton to Bideford was withdrawn on 30 April 1877, followed by that between Exeter and Crediton on 20 May 1892. The track was eventually doubled between Crediton and Copplestone, but then an agreement with the GWR, signed on 13 May 1910, to pool the receipts on competitive routes in order to avoid costly competition, obviated the need to double the line between Copplestone and Barnstaple.

The closure of the Ilfracombe line on 5 October 1970 caused the Exeter to Barnstaple line to change from main to branch status. Rationalization occurred on 17 October 1971, when the line was singled between Crediton and Copplestone. Since 1989 it has been promoted as the Tarka Line.

Until the mid-1960s Cowley Bridge Junction had double track. Slightly further on, the branch crosses the 88 yd Cowley Viaduct. Originally made of timber, it and an adjacent bridge were replaced with iron in 1874 and replaced yet again between 1965 and 1967.

Newton St Cyres (the 'Newton' was added from 1 October 1913), like most stations on the branch, had its tracks set well apart as a legacy of the broad gauge. A timber station building stood on the Up platform, which from 1930 onwards incorporated a signal-box.

Crediton, unusual in having a Brunel-type building on the LSWR, had a double footbridge at the west end of the station: one for passengers within the ticket gates; and the other for pedestrian use when the adjacent level crossing gates were closed. Following the narrowing of the gauge, the station platforms were widened to take some of the vacant space. The goods yard east of the passenger station was very busy; in 1936 4,502 trucks were received and 1,715 forwarded. There was also an LSWR slaughterhouse. In 1928 the station issued 19,788 passenger tickets, but this had declined to 8,724 in 1936. It became a Park & Ride station in 1992, with extra trains to and from Exeter. The signal-box is the only one still open on the branch, and on 16 December 1984 its levers were replaced by a panel. Beyond the station from 17 October 1971 the former double track was converted to parallel single lines; the former Down line ran to Meldon Quarry and the Up line to Barnstaple.

Yeoford had three platform roads; the Down platform was an island and had a refreshment room. The signal-box was unusually tall so that the signalman could gain a view of the goods yard on the other side of the bridge. The River Troney flowed beneath the platforms, and water from it was used for non-drinking purposes at the station and in the locomotive water columns. A porter collected spring water from the village for use in the waiting room and stationmaster's house. A mile beyond the station was Coleford Junction, where the Meldon Quarry line diverged before Crediton was made the physical junction. Copplestone, at the summit of the branch, is the first station with a building of standard North Devon Railway design. Beyond the goods shed was the LSWR slaughterhouse.

Morchard Road, another standard NDR building, had a passing loop, while Lapford was curious in that the platforms were staggered either side of a road bridge. Both platforms faced the same way and each had its own booking office. Unusually, the goods shed was on the Up platform. At the back of the station yard was the Ambrosia Dried Milk works. Built in mock-Tudor style and opened in 1928, it employed a maximum of two hundred people and offered a considerable traffic to the railway. It closed in 1970, after which the premises were used by a fertilizer firm until 1993. A slaughterhouse was situated in the arch of an overbridge.

Eggesford had a long passing loop and a long siding to an LSWR slaughterhouse, cattle pens, stores and fuel and bitumen tanks. The signal-box on the Down platform was damaged by floods, and subsidence was so severe that access could only be gained through a window. It was necessarily closed on 21 November 1967 and the loop temporarily placed out of use until a 'new' signal-box opened on 28 September 1969. The replacement box came from Ashendon Junction, west of Aylesbury. It closed on 1 December 1987, when the system was altered: a driver went to a cupboard at the end of the relevant platform, placed one token in the instrument and removed a token for the section ahead. While he was doing this, the conductor operated the level crossing barriers. Twice weekly a signal engineer placed the tablets in a tablet carrier and returned them to the issuing machine.

South Molton Road, renamed King's Nympton from 1 March 1951, had a very short passing loop. North of the station was the 64 yd Kingford Viaduct. Portsmouth Arms was an isolated station, named after a nearby inn. This commemorated the 4th Earl of Portsmouth, who built the adjacent turnpike. The station served several villages and it, too, had a short passing loop. Umberleigh was at the end of the single-track section from Copplestone, but the track beyond was singled on 21 May 1971. At one time the station had a camping coach stabled there.

Formerly oak from a saw mill adjacent to Chapelton station was supplied to the GWR, LMS and SR. Further along, the track is almost dead straight for 4 miles to Barnstaple. Three quarters of a mile beyond Chapelton the 81 yd Black Viaduct crosses the River Taw. Nearer Barnstaple there was another viaduct across the river before the GWR line from Taunton trailed in.

At one time Barnstaple Junction was very busy. In 1936 6,955 wagons were forwarded, 10,567 received and 32,263 transferred. The same year 32,287 passenger tickets were issued and 76,865 collected. As it was still much used by passengers, facilities were improved on 10 November 1982, and the main feature was a completely rebuilt and enlarged travel centre.

Around 1905 'Jubilee' class 2–4–0s Nos 618 and 638 were fitted with the Manson tablet exchange apparatus for use on nonstop runs through South Molton Road and Portsmouth Arms. Exchanges could be made at up to 50 mph. Manson's apparatus appeared in 1889 – well before Whitaker's apparatus on the Somerset & Dorset Railway – but Manson refused to patent it on humanitarian grounds, since it prevented injury to firemen during exchanges. If he had patented the device, users would have had to pay for the patent. If they could not afford it the dangerous practice of hand exchange would continue. Theoretically hand exchange was not supposed to exceed 10 mph, but it was not unknown for a driver trying to make up time to exceed this considerably.

In August 1945 locomotives of the new 'West Country' class, some named after stations on the line, were first seen between Exeter and Barnstaple. They continued to work until the demise of steam in the autumn of 1964. From 6 September of that year most Exeter–Ilfracombe trains were three-car DMUs and some other trains were hauled by diesel locomotives, both diesel-electric and diesel-hydraulic. The four-wheel class 142 'Skippers' in brown and cream livery appeared in May 1986, but as they were not satisfactory for working all Devon and Cornwall branches, from October 1987 they were transferred to Manchester and Leeds. They were replaced by older DMUs which had the advantage of having front windows through which passengers could enjoy the scenery. The main locomotive depot for the area was at Barnstaple Junction, where the timber-built shed was equipped with a small workshop. The depot closed in August 1964.

The 1887 timetable offered eight Down and seven Up trains between Exeter and Barnstaple, together with two each way on Sundays. The time taken was about 1½ hours for the 39¾ miles from Queen Street. Trains offered in 1938 were eleven Down and ten Up, with four each way on Sundays; stopping trains took about 1 hour 22 minutes. The winter 1994 timetable provided twelve services each way from Monday to Friday, nine on Saturdays and three on Sundays. Nowadays, most trains omit some stations and the time taken is just over an hour. In addition to these trains to and from Barnstaple, one Down and two Up trains operate from Exeter to Crediton on weekdays, and this is increased to three each way on Saturdays.

A note on the Regional Railways pocket timetable warns: 'After periods of heavy rainfall, flooding on local rivers may cause the temporary suspension of all or part of the Exeter to Barnstaple rail service. If this occurs a replacement road service will be introduced.'

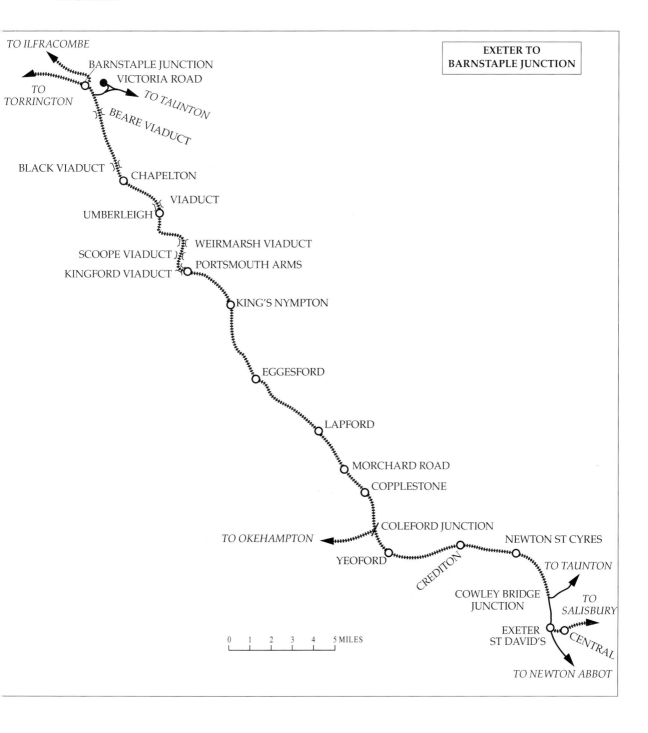

Beattie standard 0–4–2WT No. 181 at Crediton with a Down train. Built in 1863, it was rebuilt as a 2–4–0 tender engine and withdrawn in 1893. Notice the mixed gauge track, and that on the Down road the standard gauge changes from the platform side to the offside. The coach on the far left looks primitive. The siding on which it stands was lifted when the platform was lengthened, and the cattle pen was removed at the same time.

c. 1880 Author's collection

A Down train at Crediton station. Notice that the abolition of the broad gauge has allowed the platforms to be widened. Horse-drawn vehicles stand on the station approach.

c. 1910 Author's collection

The end support of the double footbridge, Crediton. The shield is inscribed 'L.&S. W. RY. 1878'.

8.8.86 Author

Gangers' motor trolley No. 68009 and trailers in the bay platform, Crediton. Note their small size when compared with the open wagon beyond.

8.8.86 Author

Nos 33025 and 33065 pass Crediton with an Up ballast train from Meldon Quarry.

25.7.94 Author

An 0–6-0 (on the right) and a 4–4–0 enter Yeoford Junction. The sign on the end of the platform canopy reads 'Refreshments'. A 5 ton crane is in the yard, loading timber.

c. 1910 Lens of Sutton

'Skipper' DMU 142019 in chocolate and cream livery approaches Morchard Road with the 12.33 Barnstaple–Exmouth service. Milepost 187½ is on the far left.

8.8.86 Author

Lapford, showing the Down platform placed between the tracks. Note the ground frame, on the left, which controlled the loop points. The bridge beyond was constructed for double track. Market pens are on the right.

c. 1960 Lens of Sutton

Pit prop wagons at Lapford outside the North Devon & North Cornwall Farmers Ltd building, formerly the Ambrosia factory.

8.8.86 Author

The replacement signal-box at Eggesford, which came from Ashendon Junction.

8.8.86 Author

Sprinter 150253 arrives at Eggesford with the 11.07 Barnstaple–Exeter train. The guard walks forward to operate the lifting barriers. Notice the weeds in the track near the platform ramp.

25.7.94 Author

The tablet instrument in the box at the end of the Up platform at Eggesford.

25.7.94 Author

John Norman, Rail Operator II, slides the tablets from the instruments on a carrier.

25.7.94 Author

John Norman, Rail Operator II, has a full carrier to return to Barnstaple.

25.7.94 Author

The very attractive former station building at King's Nympton.

8.8.86 Author

'West Country' class 4–6–2 No. 34028 *Eddystone* (72A, Exmouth Junction) with a Down train at Portsmouth Arms. The locomotive has been preserved by A.J.R. Burchill & Son Ltd at Sellindge, Kent.

c. 1958 M.E.J. Deane

Sprinter 150253 at Portsmouth Arms working the 09.24 Exmouth–Barnstaple service. Note the 'Crystal Palace'-type waiting shelter and the tubs of flowers.

25.7.94 Author

An exceptionally long kissing gate at Chapelton, to allow bicycles and handcarts to be taken through.

8.8.86 Author

The arrival at Barnstaple of the first train from Crediton. It has just passed through a triumphal arch, while another can be seen to the left of the station building.

12.7.1854 Courtesy *Illustrated London News*

A broad gauge train at Barnstaple, ready to leave for Exeter. It is headed by 2–2–2 *Tite*, formerly Bristol & Gloucester Railway No. 5 *Gloucester* (and subsequently MR No. 261/361/461), built by Bury, Curtis & Kennedy in 1844. Note the shunting horse. A telegraph post and wires are in the foreground.

c. 1858 Author's collection

The broad gauge 2–4–0 goods engine *Creedy*, built in 1855. Note that in addition to the name being painted on the four-wheel tender, it is on a rectangular plate fixed to the boiler. *Creedy* was one of the two broad gauge engines retained when, owing to most trains being standard gauge, the other broad gauge stock was abandoned. *Creedy* was eventually withdrawn in 1877.

c. 1870 Author's collection

At Barnstaple locomotive shed M7 class 0–4–4T No. 30 is on the right and No. 48 on the left. Notice that a GWR brake van is coupled to No. 30. The water pipe is lagged to prevent freezing, and the workman is shovelling clinker.

21.7.25 H.C. Casserley

HOLIDAY RUNABOUT TICKETS
A WEEK'S UNLIMITED TRAVEL

During 1959 Holiday Runabout Tickets will be issued from 26th April to 31st October. They can be obtained at any station shown on the maps of this handbill and are valid for seven days from date of issue.

JOINT AREA No. 7
Ilfracombe, Barnstaple,
Torrington, Dulverton,
Exeter, Newton Abbot.

AREA No. 13
Ilfracombe, Barnstaple,
Okehampton, Exeter,
Exmouth.

EACH AREA
18/6
SECOND CLASS ONLY

Tickets are also issued in conjunction with the above areas, permitting trips on Messrs. P. & A. Campbell's Bristol Channel Steamers from Ilfracombe to Lundy Island. Combined charge for each Area (7A and 13A) 31/- 2nd Class.

Passengers should enquire at stations for information regarding dates and times of steamer sailings (weather and circumstances permitting).

CHILDREN 3 YEARS AND UNDER 14 HALF-FARE
Holiday Runabout Tickets are not available by "CORNISH RIVIERA" Express trains, nor on Road Motors or on the Exmouth & Starcross Ferry.

For Area 11 and
other charges
see overleaf

Details on a hand bill for Runabout tickets.

1959 Author's collection

129

Coleford to Meldon Quarry

The Okehampton Railway Act of 17 July 1862 authorized a line from Coleford Junction to be worked by the LSWR. Sharpe & Sons did not start the contract until 31 March 1864, when the Countess of Portsmouth cut the first sod at Coleford. A special was run on 28 October 1865 from Yeoford to North Tawton, drawn by *Tiny*, the contractor's engine. The single line was opened to the public on 1 November 1865, and celebrations included a dinner.

On 8 January 1867 the line was extended to Okehampton Road (renamed Belstone Corner on 3 October 1871 and then Sampford Courtenay on 1 January 1872). Okehampton itself was reached on 3 October 1871, the proprietor of the White Hart Hotel giving a dinner in the goods shed to the navvies. An Act of 29 June 1865 changed the name of the company to the Devon & Cornwall Railway and permitted an extension to the South Devon Railway at Lydford on 17 June 1870. The Devon & Cornwall Railway was absorbed into the LSWR in 1872, and the line opened to Meldon and Lydford on 12 October 1874.

The line between Yeoford Junction and Meldon Junction, including Meldon Viaduct, was doubled between 16 May 1877 and 1 November 1879. Okehampton to Bere Alston closed on 6 May 1968 and the shuttle passenger service from Exeter to Okehampton was withdrawn on 5 June 1972. A limited service sponsored by Devon County Council ceased after 1986.

Coleford Junction signal-box closed on 17 October 1971, when the lines from Crediton were made parallel single tracks. The Meldon branch was singled on the same date. From the junction the line climbs at 1 in 97, steepening to 1 in 80 before Bow station, which was built of granite, with round-headed windows. The climb continues and then a short descent is made before North Tawton, where the station was similar to that at Bow. West of Bow are four straight miles – unusual on a British railway. The station footbridge from North Tawton is preserved on the Mid-Hants Railway. The track at North Tawton station is now 2 ft above the platforms, as the rail level has been raised to allow an underbridge to be lifted, enabling tall lorries to pass under it. Beyond North Tawton is North Tawton Viaduct, 63 yd long, then the line climbs at 1 in 77 to Sampford Courtenay. This was another station with an LSWR slaughterhouse. Almost 3 miles beyond is the 80 yd Fatherford Viaduct, built of stone.

Okehampton station was rebuilt by the SR in the 1920s, and the glass canopies made the platforms unusually light. It was busy, as trains with portions for Plymouth and North Cornwall were divided and combined there, and the goods shed had fourteen bays. When additional sidings were laid on land hewn from the hillside, a locomotive shed was built on the spoil, which formed an embankment. The station, at 750 ft above sea level, stood above the town. In 1909 a military dock was built at the south end of the station to handle Dartmoor range artillery traffic. The track at the dock was lifted on 2 March 1966.

Beyond Okehampton the line to Meldon Quarry, singled on 22 March 1970, climbs at 1 in 77. When the line was built in the 1870s, a siding was laid to Meldon Quarry 'for the removal of small amounts of stone by an engine stationed at our Okehampton shed'. In 1897 the LSWR purchased this quarry and in 1905 bought sixteen 40 ton bogie hopper wagons – very large vehicles for the period – to convey ballast. The quarry's output in 1913 was 125,200 tons. It was not Dartmoor granite, but hard limestone. In the 1930s, eight to nine ballast trains each of ten 40 ton hopper wagons, were despatched weekly. Passenger trains were not normally held up by blasting, but goods trains were not infrequently stopped at Meldon Junction or Okehampton, and the Meldon Quarry signalman had to take shelter; blast screens were erected over his signal-box windows.

After crushing, the stone was graded into permanent way ballast, shovel packing and concrete aggregate. The crushing plant caught fire on 1 March 1908, damaging the plant's timber framing. In 1979 a new layout was introduced to cope with increased traffic, the output of 300,000 tons a year making it the largest rail-owned quarry in Britain.

A small community grew around the quarry and to provide transport to and from the outside world, Meldon Quarry Halt opened around 1890. Unusually narrow, it was only one paving stone in width. The pay clerk alighted there each Friday and quarrymen's wives used the train for their Saturday shopping trips to Okehampton. The halt necessarily closed when passenger trains were withdrawn. In 1946 three Austin ambulances, purchased from the Ministry of Supply at £230 each, were converted to personnel carriers and worked three routes around the area taking workmen to the quarry. Although a scar on the landscape, the quarry provides employment. In 1994 Network SouthEast sold it to Camas, but this has made little difference to traffic. Normally three trains leave daily, usually worked by two class 37s.

Immediately beyond the quarry is Meldon Viaduct, which consists of six spans each of 85½ ft, with a maximum height over the River Okement of 130 ft. The wrought-iron Warren girder spans are supported on wrought-iron lattice piers, making it one of the very few all-metal viaducts in Great Britain. When the line was doubled in 1879 a similar, but independent, viaduct was built alongside. It is on a 30 chain curve.

The first permanent quarry shunter at Meldon was SR No. 225S, allocated in the mid-1920s. It was ex-SECR No. 313, a Manning Wardle 0–4–0ST. Towards the end of the '30s T class 0–6–0T No. 500S was the quarry shunter; in the '50s it was G6 class 0–6–0T No. 272, re-numbered DS 3152, then USA 0–6–0T DS 234 and in 1966 an 08 diesel electric. In the early days the Meldon engine returned to Exmouth Junction shed, but as this was uneconomic, the engine shed at Okehampton was lengthened to hold the quarry engine. Eventually a timber and corrugated iron shed was built at Meldon itself, though it was later replaced by a concrete building.

The timber engine shed at Okehampton opened in 1890 and was doubled in length around 1919. It was destroyed by fire on 7 June 1920, causing damage to the two engines inside. The blaze was started by a careless railway employee. The shed was replaced by a long single-road structure of concrete block walls with an asbestos roof. In 1947 a new 70 ft turntable was installed.

To begin with, in 1865, six trains ran each way between Yeoford and Okehampton Road. In 1887 there were ten trains to Okehampton and eight from, with three each way on Sundays. By 1922 the number of trains had increased to fourteen daily each way and still three on Sundays. In 1961 the number of weekday trains was about the same (twelve Down and thirteen Up), but six ran each way on Sundays.

One unusual mishap occurred on the line. On 30 March 1875 a passenger train from Yeoford, headed by an engine running tender-first, left North Tawton and descended to North Tawton Viaduct. As it climbed the 1 in 77 beyond, the driver realized that his train was missing. Wisely, he proceeded in case the train caught up and crashed into the engine. Later he stopped and sent the fireman back with a handlamp, the engine following him. As there was no sign of the train when he reached the viaduct, he let the fireman ride on the front buffer beam. Then, to his horror, the driver saw the leading wheels of his train reflecting the light from the fireman's lamp. He stopped his engine, but failed to reverse it before the carriages struck. Three passengers were injured. The guard was completely unaware that his train was engineless. When the coaches slowed down, ran back, stopped and moved forward again, he had merely assumed that the driver was trying to get a better run at the gradient.

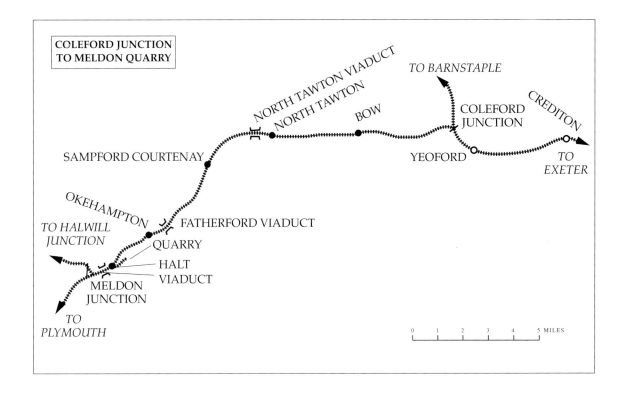

A basket of rabbits at North Tawton.

c. 1905 Author's collection

The military dock at the south end of Okehampton station layout. There are passenger coaches, two horse boxes and about twenty cattle trucks, used for the less valuable animals. Note that the main line climbing towards Meldon is at a higher level than the sidings.

c. 1914 Lens of Sutton

L11 class 4–4–0 No. 439 outside Okehampton shed.

18.7.48 South Western Circle Wessex Collection

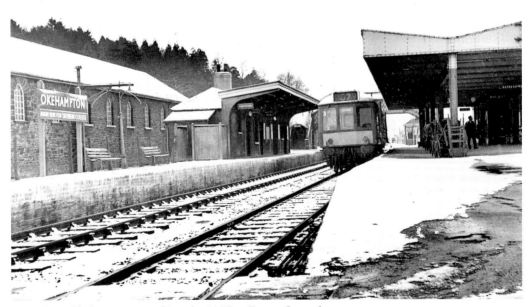

A DMU at Okehampton, working the 14.35 to Exeter Central.

28.12.68 E. Wilmshurst

The loading plant at Meldon Quarry.

15.5.65 South Western Circle Wessex Collection

G6 class 0–6–0T No. DS 682 in the new locomotive shed at Meldon Quarry.

c. 1961 Lens of Sutton

An Up express from Plymouth passes Meldon Quarry Halt.

19.7.58 Hugh Davies

An Adams 4–4–0 crossing the double track Meldon Viaduct.

Date unknown. M.E.J. Deane collection

The Lynton & Barnstaple Railway

Back in 1895 Jones Brothers of Lynton operated two four-horse coaches each way between Barnstaple and Lynton, covering the 18 miles in 2 hours 50 minutes. A standard gauge railway would have been costly to build over such hilly terrain, but a narrow gauge line of 1 ft 11½ in was anticipated as curves could be much sharper – a definite advantage when following contours. This would also lower construction costs by two-thirds.

An Act of 27 June 1895 authorized the Lynton & Barnstaple Railway, and Lady Newnes cut the first sod on 17 September 1895 at Shambleway, near Lynbridge. The contract for construction was let to J. Nuttall. The cost of blasting through rock, which the company's consulting engineer did not expect, bankrupted the contractor. However, the line was eventually finished and in May 1898 Col. Yorke carried out the Board of Trade inspection. The railway was formally opened on 11 May by Sir George and Lady Newnes and opened to the public five days later. That year, when being interviewed by the writer of an article in the *Railway Magazine*, Newnes said: 'I believe that Lynton has for some time enjoyed the distinction of being the only place in England extensively visited by tourists, despite the fact that it is twenty miles from any railway station . . . It has been the regular thing in July and August to see twenty or thirty coaches and *chars-a-bancs* from Ilfracombe crowd into Lynton between 11 and 12 o'clock in the morning.'

In March 1923 the SR bought the LBR for £39,267. The costs were broken down as follows: line £31,061; four engines and seventeen coaches £7,307; twenty-four goods vehicles, land and buildings £899. The company was not acquired under the Railways Act 1921. The company's best year financially had been 1913, when gross receipts were £9,668 and working expenses £6,640. For 1922 the figures were £14,511 and £14,948 respectively.

Despite improvements made by its new owners, the line was unable to compete with the growth of road traffic, and sales of tickets dropped dramatically from 72,000 in 1925 to 32,000 in 1934. In 1935 a decision had to be made about whether to undertake the expense of permanent way renewals or to close the line. The latter course was adopted. A meeting was held at Barnstaple to try to reverse the decision, but the fact that all the railway's supporters had travelled from Lynton by car rather ruined their case.

Yeo and *Lew* headed nine coaches on the last train on 29 September 1935. The rolling stock and materials were auctioned in the carriage shed at the Pilton depot on 13 November. The five locomotives made £34–£52 each; the carriages £10–£13 10s each; a 4 ton four-wheeled open wagon £3 15s; two 4½ ton vans £30 and £29; Lynton signal-box and signals £7. The track was withdrawn at 2s a yard, for sale by private treaty. The turntable was sold to the Romney, Hythe & Dymchurch Railway. One locomotive chimney was fitted to a steam roller owned by Murch & Sons, Umberleigh, and worked at Barnstaple until November 1958. Following the closure of the LBR, Southern National buses operating from Lynton to Barnstaple were constructed to carry luggage such as parcels, milk churns, and even sheep and goats, in addition to passengers.

The LBR and LSWR erected a joint station at Barnstaple (later called Barnstaple Town), to replace the LSWR's Barnstaple Quay station. The narrow gauge used one side of the platform and the standard gauge the other. Just beyond Braunton Road level crossing, a trailing siding led to a wharf on the River Yeo. Beyond Pilton Road level crossing was the railway's headquarters. Here were an engine shed, carriage shed, goods shed and repair shop. The turntable was provided so that the wear on wheels could be equalized.

Snapper Halt, opened in February 1903, had a low platform, as did all the other stations on the line except Barnstaple, and a mere line of bricks defined the edge. Just beyond, at Collar Bridge over the River Yeo, began an 8 mile climb on a gradient of 1 in 50. Chelfham Viaduct, made of yellow brick, and with eight 42 ft spans 70 ft above the road, was the railway's largest engineering feature and is now Grade II listed. Beyond, in a tunnel of trees, was Chelfham, the LBR's most picturesque station. It had a crossing loop like all the other stations, but, unusually, a goods siding bisected the Down platform. This was a feature also found at Bratton Fleming.

Lancey Brook Viaduct consisted of eight 15 ft steel spans on masonry piers. The rail level was at a maximum height of 28 ft. Bratton Fleming had an ivy-covered waiting room, its mossy roof set against a rock face. The Down loop was converted into a siding on 16 June 1931. Approximately midway between Bratton Fleming and Blackmoor the line rose at its maximum gradient of 1 in 29. Blackmoor had the usual crossing loop. Parracombe Halt opened in May 1903 and initially was only used on Fridays, market day. Woody Bay marked the summit of the line, 980 ft above sea level. Caffyns Halt opened in 1907 to serve golf links. Lynton, 750 ft above sea level, had a main and a bay platform. Adjacent was a small engine shed. The station was carefully placed so as to be invisible from Lynton or Lynmouth and thus did not impinge on the picturesque environment, but its inaccessibility, 250 ft above the town, in later years proved to be a misjudgement.

The LBR purchased three 27¼ ton 2–6–2Ts from Manning, Wardle & Co., and named them *Yeo*, *Exe* and *Taw*. It then needed another locomotive, but because British builders could not supply owing to a strike coupled with an ordering boom, the railway purchased a Baldwin 2–4–2T from the USA. Although officially named *Lyn*, it was always known to the staff as 'Yankee'. Sent over in crates, it was assembled at Barnstaple in 1898. All the engines were painted dark green. Although the line was fenced, the engines carried cowcatchers. When the SR took over, it felt that an additional locomotive was needed and so ordered *Lew* from Manning, Wardle.

Passenger rolling stock consisted of seventeen bogie carriages on roller bearings, and these vehicles tended to rock excessively. One of the coaches now runs on the Festiniog Railway. The livery was lake on the lower panels, with the upper finished in white. Built at the Bristol Wagon & Carriage Works, some had a central compartment, which was left open above waist level for passengers to enjoy the view. There was also a first-class observation carriage with end windows. The coaches were acetylene lit, with generators at the end of each coach. The SR provided steam heating in 1933 and when this was in use, goods wagons were placed at the rear, instead of in front of the coaches. Freight was carried in twenty-five wagons painted light grey, and, unlike contemporary main-line wagons, these were all fitted with vacuum brakes.

Trains were allowed about 92 minutes for the journey of 19¼ miles. This was not excessive, considering the gradients and that mixed trains were worked, shunting goods wagons at several stations. This gave an average speed of about 15 mph. The five trains provided in 1898 fell to three in 1910, plus two on Fridays, and in 1924 increased to four trains plus one on Mondays, Fridays and Saturdays. In 1932 an 'express' was introduced, calling only at Blackmoor and Bratton Fleming. This covered the distance to Barnstaple in 80 minutes.

Interesting day excursions were run from South Wales using the paddle steamer to Ilfracombe, a train to Barnstaple and Lynton, then a horse coach to Ilfracombe or Minehead, and finally the paddle steamer home.

As on many branches, interesting incidents occurred. One engineman, after shunting at Chelfham, drove on to Barnstaple without his train and had the humiliation of having to return for it. In dry summers there was a water shortage at Lynton station and the public was requested to refrain from using the lavatories. The Revd J.F. Chanter of Parracombe used to scatter seed from the carriage window in the railway's early days to help beautify the scars caused by its construction.

The LBR ran the first railway motor bus feeder service in Great Britain. From the opening of the line, a horse-drawn coach operated from Ilfracombe to Blackmoor station, but early in 1903 Sir George Newnes decided to motorize the service. He purchased two 22-seat 16 h.p. Milnes Daimler motor wagonettes and began the service on 30 May 1903. Following difficulties with the police, when vehicles were found 'speeding above 8 mph', the two buses were sold to the GWR, which used them to inaugurate a Helston to Lizard service on 17 August 1903.

The Lynton & Barnstaple Railway Association has been formed to re-open at least part of the line. In January 1995 it announced that Woody Bay station had been purchased and a planning application would be submitted for relaying the line between Woody Bay and Parracombe. Following this initial development there would be significant, but not insuperable, obstructions to extending the line in both directions.

No. 188 *Lew* at Barnstaple Town. Standard gauge track can be seen on the right.

c. 1930 Lens of Sutton

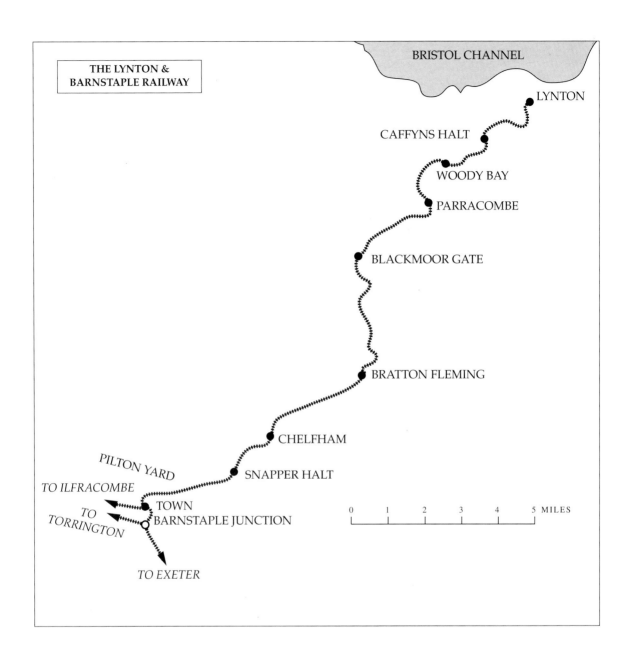

THE LYNTON &
BARNSTAPLE RAILWAY

BRISTOL CHANNEL

LYNTON

CAFFYNS HALT

WOODY BAY

PARRACOMBE

BLACKMOOR GATE

BRATTON FLEMING

CHELFHAM

PILTON YARD

SNAPPER HALT

TO ILFRACOMBE

TO
TORRINGTON

TOWN

BARNSTAPLE JUNCTION

TO EXETER

0   1   2   3   4   5 MILES

Unloading *Yeo* from a standard gauge wagon at Barnstaple Town, using traversing jacks.

1898 Author's collection

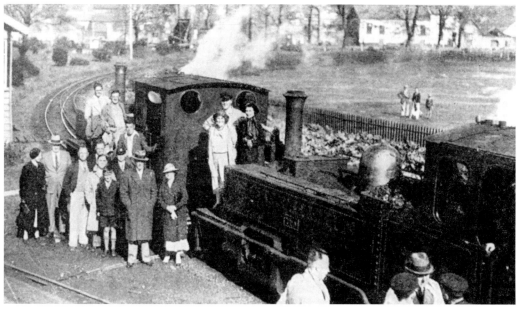

The last train to Lynton about to leave Barnstaple Town. *Lew* is to the left and *Yeo* to the right.

29.9.35 Author's collection

Yeo (left) and *Exe* (right) at Pilton Yard. Notice the rather flimsy fence in the foreground. The locomotive shed is to the left and the carriage shed to the right.

11.5.1898 Author's collection

The simple, yet attractive, Snapper Halt, which opened in February 1903. The view is looking in the Up direction.

c. 1930 Lens of Sutton

2–4–2T *Lyn* has stopped in the Yeo Valley with a
two-coach train, presumably for this photograph.
c. 1935 Author's collection

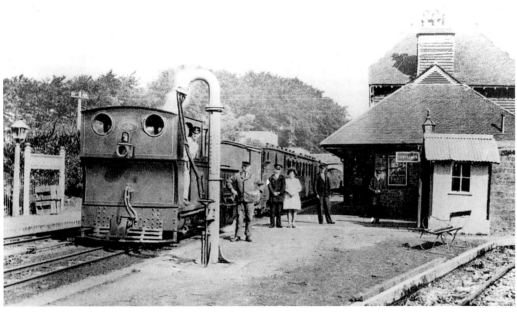

A Manning, Wardle locomotive heading an Up train takes water at Blackmoor Gate. The water
tank can be seen above the first coach.

c. 1930 Author's collection

Yeo with the reporters' train at Woody Bay.

16.3.1898 Author's collection

Lady Newnes cuts the ribbons for the arrival of the first train at Lynton.

11.5.1898 Author's collection

Yeo heading a trial train at Collar Bridge. Notice the slender fencing.

1898 Author's collection

Taw at Lynton. Note the first-class observation coach open above waist level. In inclement weather canvas blinds were drawn across. The contractor's plant in the foreground indicates that the photograph was taken before the station opened.

14.3.1898 Author's collection

Lynton, looking towards the buffers. Note the telegraph wires attached to the top of the lamp-post.
c. 1935 Lens of Sutton

Lynton & Barnstaple Railway Co.

The Lynton Station Water Supply has failed, and the public are requested to refrain from using the Station lavatories.

By Order.

An unwelcome notice which sometimes appeared at Lynton in the summer.
Date unknown Author's collection